WHAT OTHERS SAY

In her book, Chris Timmins shares her story, describing how her faith in God, insight, and fortitude moved her from victim to victor. Chris' journey inspires us to meet our own challenges and come through them triumphantly.

— Gloria Lewis, colleague

Chris Timmins is a role model educator who redefines ability.... Her guiding spirit has benefited teens for more than 30 years, and her colleagues will tell you, "She no longer leaves footprints in the sand, but leaves imprints on the hearts and minds of all whom she has taught and touched."

— Eagle Spirit Award, Sharp Hospital

She has inspired others to overcome challenges with grace and a positive attitude...she brought her contagious enthusiasm into the classroom.

— Russ and Peggy Stai, parents of three former students

Chris' ministry and spirit is a testament to the ability of God to bring goodness out of even the most tragic of events or circumstances. Her words and message will inspire and bless the reader. I'm thrilled she wrote this book!

— The Rev. Suzanne E. Watson

I learned to keep a perspective on what is really important—family and friends... and to keep a positive, upbeat outlook on life.

— Marge Cole, school administrator

The Up Side of Down

Christine Ostertag Timmins

Cover logo and photography by Jamie Moore Chapel
Cover design by Paul Thompson
Interior design by Tim Brittain
"Braided Streams" graphic by James Jenkins
Editing by David S. Cohen

Braided Streams
San Diego, CA 92124

www.BraidedStreams.com

Library of Congress Control Number: 2012910759

ISBN: 978-0-9669637-3-1

Printed In Korea

CONTENTS

ACKNOWLEDGMENTS

Many of the women below came into my life when it was turned *Up Side Down*, and have been with me throughout the journey. They were instrumental in setting examples for me in the ways they live their own lives and in the ways they have helped me through mine. Many thanks and much appreciation to the following people:

Listeners, Encouragers, and Editors

Dr. Donna Brooks, MD
Jan Daugherty
BJ Gallagher
Gloria Lewis
Shirley Moore
Janet Allen Shaw
Mary Thompson

Mentors on my Journey

Cathy Conheim, LCSW
Joni Eareckson Tada, author, speaker
Jill Kinmont, first California teacher with quadriplegia
Dr. Kris Laverty, PhD
Rev. Patricia Moore

Design and Technical Assistance

Cover logo and photography by Jamie Moore Chapel, photographer
Cover design by Paul Thompson, photographer
Editing by David S. Cohen
Interior design by Tim Brittain
Title by Judy Timmins

INTRODUCTION

By Cathy Conheim,
Therapist and author of *Henry's World,*
What's the Matter with Henry? and *What About Me?*

Chris Timmins is an amazing woman. Thirty-three years ago, she and her husband were preparing to leave San Diego and move to Oregon. That bright, sunny morning while they were finishing up last-minute details, Chris was feeling nostalgic and decided to take one last spin around Fiesta Island in her beloved little BMW convertible. What happened to her on that drive is still a bit of a mystery. She could feel herself getting dizzy and tried to pull over to the side of the road, but she lost control and crashed into a cement road divider. When she regained consciousness in the hospital, she was a quadriplegic. Her whole life was turned upside down.

During the next 30 years, Chris had several other struggles — getting her job back to teach high school, gaining strength in one hand to be able to feed herself and write again, being able to drive a specially-equipped van, living independently and surviving breast cancer — to name a few.

Chris not only rose to meet each personal and professional crisis, she triumphed over them. She was finally able to convince the San Diego School District that her presence in the classroom would greatly enrich the education of her students. Her message to the kids: **It is not the events of your life that determine the kind of future you'll have. It is how you respond to those events that gives you quality in your life.** Chris was, and is, the living embodiment of that message.

Many people suffer paralysis, not only physically, but spiritually or emotionally. The message of Chris' phenomenal life: **We are NOT paralyzed as people — there is always something we can do, no matter how big the problem. By taking action, any action, people can overcome their own personal sense of paralysis.**

So many times people get overwhelmed in the face of their problems — financial trouble, personal struggles, family issues — it is easy to give up and give in. We do nothing because we don't believe there's anything we *can* do. We don't reach out to help others because we feel like we can't even help ourselves. But Chris' life — and the lives of others she writes about in this book — encourages us to banish such feelings of hopelessness and helplessness. When you read about what a wonderful life she's created for herself, and how many thousands of others she's helped along the way, you'll never let despair and doubt darken your door again.

Life is not the way it's supposed to be.
It's the way it is.
The way you deal with it is what makes the difference.

— Virginia Satir

The way I see it, if you want the rainbow,
you got to put up with the rain.

— Dolly Parton

We grow through adversity. We need not seek it out;
we can all look back at moments when our lives
were in utter chaos, desolation, and despair.
Growth comes when we respond to adversity
by stretching just an edge beyond our talent and experience.

— Dr. Robert D. Wald

BRAIDED STREAMS

Running Through My Life

Welcome to my Braided Streams—pieces and passages of my life tied and woven together into what I hope are coherent strands of experience. In this book, I will be sharing lessons I've learned over the past 34 years in my wheelchair. It is a compilation of intertwining themes running through my life.

I like the image of *streams* because, for me, it symbolizes fluidity and serves as a metaphor for my life's journey. The themes that I have incorporated in the following chapters include:

Family & Friends ~ God's Love & Grace ~ Choice & Responsibility
Patience & Acceptance ~ Hope & Joy ~ Celebration & Victory ~ Connection & Community
Gratitude & Thankfulness ~ Purpose & Passion

These streams have sometimes trickled over a rocky streambed, leaving me feeling stuck and depressed. At other times, they rush over mossy soil and move forward effortlessly. Most importantly, my braided streams are deep and strong enough to carry the intertwining themes and lessons I write about, but shallow enough to let me see them clearly and reflect on them as I am ready. I picture them in my mind like this:

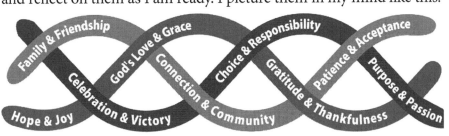

My story: I am retired after 39 years of teaching high school (32 years from a wheelchair) in San Diego, California. Teaching really was a wonderful career for me, and I enjoyed it up to and including my last day. I tried to be a role model and push my students to reach their full potential in all they accomplished. More than teaching subject content, I feel my greatest strength was in recognizing the best in them while being supportive and encouraging.

> *We do not believe in ourselves until someone reveals*
> *that deep inside us something is valuable,*
> *worth listening to, worthy of our trust, sacred to our touch.*
>
> — e.e. cummings

I especially value the times my students have shared with me what influence my class or I had on their lives....

———

My challenges began when I broke my neck in a car accident that left me quadriplegic (little or no movement in all four limbs). An unexpected divorce came four years later. Then, 12 years after that, I was diagnosed with breast cancer. With the help of a mastectomy, chemotherapy, and radiation, I am now a survivor of over 20 years. But this isn't my whole story....

Although there have been other trials and challenges along the way, I have been fortunate in feeling God's presence and guidance since I was very young. I have had my share of down days, but my faith has always enabled me to remain hopeful and positive.

I think most people have some type of pain or adversity in their lives. It is my hope that some of my experiences will connect with you in new or unique ways. If my journey and the lessons I have learned can, even in the smallest ways, help others to overcome their challenges, pursue their goals and dreams, and find joy, my purpose in writing this book will be fulfilled.

Some days you feel life is on the upswing;
other days it's flat.
Sometimes you sense the miracle in your life;
other times life seems very ordinary.
Are you energized today to meet a challenge head-on?
Or do you feel tired and trapped?
Life's circumstances can make you feel like a yo-yo,
but don't allow the "ups and downs" to get you down.
Commit to God to fight the good fight...
finish the race...keep the faith.

— Joni Eareckson Tada,
from *Pearls of Great Price*

THE ACCIDENT

Life for me has not always been full of challenges; in fact, it had been care-free. I was 28 and had been happily married to my college love for almost eight years. I had a beautiful home, was driving my dream car, and had a career that I very much enjoyed. We had big plans, high hopes, and shared visions for a wonderful, fulfilling, and long life together. Then — THE ACCIDENT.

It was 1978. I was driving around Mission Bay in beautiful, sunny San Diego. I selfishly wanted one more day at the beach while my husband Mike stayed at home packing up the house for our move. I didn't really want to leave San Diego or my job as a high school teacher, but I did want to start a family and that was only going to happen (according to my husband) if we moved to a smaller town which would be a better environment to raise kids. Our plan was to move to Bend, Oregon, where my sister was living.

After enjoying my last afternoon on the sand, I packed up and headed for home. At a left-hand turn lane, I began to feel cramps and nausea. I remember thinking, "There are cars lined up behind me and skateboarders and people on bikes all around me; I can't just turn off my car here. I'll make it through this turn and pull over." When the light turned green, I started my left turn. Then everything went black — I have no memory after that, I just know that my car jumped in and out of the bike lane and didn't stop until I hit a cement embankment. I opened my eyes long enough to know that my face was on top of the gear-shift knob.

I woke up again lying on an emergency room table where they were cutting my dress and swimsuit off. I was asked my name, the date, and who was president. Thankfully, I was able to pass that preliminary test. The next time I woke up was after surgery on my neck — a laminectomy which allowed my spinal cord to swell without doing more damage. I was looking up at the ceiling from a Stryker frame bed (which flipped me from my back to my stomach like making toast over an open fire). My neck was in traction so I could not move it or see from side to side.

I could move only my eyelashes....

I could hear my husband's voice beside me. Mike explained what had happened in my accident, about the surgery, and about how I had broken my neck at an angle at cervical levels 4-5-6. I heard him tell me the prognosis of my recovery: I would have no movement below my shoulders. I tried to make meaning from his words. I'm not sure how long it took me to understand what he was saying. Maybe hours, maybe days, maybe weeks. More truly, it took years.

There were no trauma hospitals in 1978, so after a week in a tiny beachside hospital, I was moved, via ambulance, to Kaiser Hospital. While there, not quite two weeks after my accident, I was fitted with a plaster body cast attached to a "halo" cast. It was screwed into my skull in four places. I noticed that they were using a Craftsman drill from Sears, and I remember thinking that it felt more like I was in a carpenter's workshop than a hospital. How strange the things we remember!

I also knew that my parents were outside the room hearing my screams. The pain was unbearable, and yet I kept thinking, "It's my mom's 50th birthday! What kind of gift is this?"

I remained in that hospital for one month. Then I was transferred to Sharp Rehabilitation Center here in San Diego.

REHABILITATION AND RECOVERY

Physical and Emotional

This is not the end. It is not even the beginning of the end.
But, it is, perhaps, the end of the beginning.

— Sir Winston Churchill

My husband and my parents chose Sharp Rehab for its good reputation and proximity to home. No matter how good the care was, however, having the support of family and friends nearby was the most important factor in my recovery. Visitors were my lifeline to my "life as I knew it before." As much as I enjoyed everyone who came, ironically, I often found myself in the position of being the person doing the cheering up! Oftentimes when friends would enter my room, especially if it were the first time, they would burst into tears, and I would then spend the next several minutes letting them know that I was okay and all would be well…. Their shock should have been a sign to me about the gravity of my condition, but I was not thinking ahead at that time. My neck was broken; when I'd first awakened after my surgery, I was unable to move anything. And I had thought all would be okay? Clearly, I had not grasped the reality of my situation!

I had no way of knowing what the real effects of this accident were going to be on my life and my future. My life was turned upside down in the blink of an eye. I think God had me in a protective bubble, letting in only as much information as I was able to take in at any given time. It was probably a blessing that I was trying to make others feel good as it kept me from feeling deeply and utterly depressed. I was undoubtedly in a state of ignorant bliss.

In order to get me out of bed, into a wheelchair, and in position to begin therapy, my body was placed in a 40-pound plaster cast from my shoulders to my hips with four metal bars going up to the *halo* around my head. I couldn't turn my head and I was too heavy for only one person to maneuver my body. When I was moved from bed to wheelchair, a hoist called a Hoyer lift was brought in. A sling was fitted around my body and under each leg. I felt like a car engine being hoisted out of the frame. I had no control of my legs which were indecently spread open. It was embarrassing; I was often dressed only in a hospital gown, and I felt stripped of all dignity. Since I couldn't physically cover myself, I felt myself shrinking within, trying to make my body invisible while at the same time trying to block the whole experience from my mind. Instead of blocking it out, however, it has remained one of many difficult memories — and it was just the beginning of a long and emotionally painful journey.

There were both good times and lonely times during the six months I spent at Rehab. The nurses and aides were compassionate, helpful, and often very funny — this made the days go more quickly. I vividly remember one night when my two favorite nursing assistants, Joanie and Bobbi, were trying to put a rapidly-made foam splint on my hand. It was supposed to gently encourage my fingers to curl. I was told that tightly curled fingers would benefit me later if I could hold a pen or a fork. (No one knows why my fingers never curled, but I'm glad now.) Back to my story: this contraption had so much Velcro and so many straps that the two of them could not for the life of them figure out how to strap it on. After many attempts, we were laughing so hard we cried.

During my physical and occupational therapy appointments, the therapists were all skillful as they patiently taught me how to strengthen and move the few muscles that could still receive directions from my brain. Because of the location of the break in my neck, messages from my brain could no longer reach the majority of my other muscles, therefore, the paralysis in all four of my limbs.

The section of the hospital where I was staying held only 40 patients divided between spinal cord injuries (SCI), stroke victims, and traumatic brain injuries. It was hard for me to identify with most of the other patients. They were typically young boys who had broken their necks or backs doing something athletic or crazy; others were unable to communicate easily due to strokes or brain damage. There was, however, one married man who was going through almost the exact same struggles that I was — broken neck, life turned upside down and a spouse he was trying to hang on to. We had so much in common and each of us understood what the other was going through. Because of that, we tried to be assigned as roommates — but that was a "no-no" — even in the '70s. Ironic! What kind of mischief could we get into, paralyzed as we both were!

Instead, my roommate was a "little person" who had been one of the original Munchkins in *The Wizard of Oz*. I don't remember her injury — only that she screamed all the time. Luckily her husband, also a Munchkin in the movie (and now in his '80s), was fun to talk to.

There were wonderful employees and a few patients with whom I could talk and share, but for the most part, this experience was a chilly blast to my heart. I had been plucked out of my comfortable, happy life and placed in this health "institution" for six months. Every day I needed somebody, a stranger, to bathe and dress me (no place for modesty), transfer me into my wheelchair and wheel me down to therapy. Someone else would pick me up from therapy and wheel me to lunch and feed me. It felt sterile and cold. I was near tears on a regular basis and couldn't wait each day until Mike came to visit after work. He and I went to counseling and group meetings. Counselors and therapists were friendly and polite, but I couldn't help wondering, "How do they really know what I am going through, or will go through?" We were given information about how to live our lives — find caregivers, make structural changes to the bathroom, and in general, how to make our home wheelchair accessible. There were also sessions on intimacy and some fairly graphic videos on how other couples were coping with paralysis. Everything was very clinical and a bit surreal, since I had not yet begun living my life as a quadriplegic. It seemed all the information was for someone else, not me.

Nights were especially difficult; I was beyond sad and lonely. I frequently felt desperate, but I didn't really know what for. Oftentimes I called Mike to come over in the middle of the night and sit with me while I cried. I can't even imagine how he must have felt.... He came to comfort me, although he had likely left a warm, comfortable bed. I took this as a sign of love and caring, yet I wonder now whether tiny seeds of resentment were being planted then.

All in all, my visitors made the experience tolerable. They brought me cards, Bible studies, flowers, yummy desserts, music, love and laughter. They were the sunlight against the stark reality of my life in Rehab.

—⟨⟨⟨⟩⟩⟩—

The goal of my rehabilitation was to find any little movement we could in my body, strengthen it and then determine what tasks of daily living I could do for myself. It seemed at first as though we were searching for a needle in a haystack. In fact, they used a needle test to lightly prick my skin to find my level of sensation. I had no movement or feeling below my neck. The nurses sat me in my chair each day, but I could do nothing. As lifeless as my body was, I was at least aware of how fortunate I was to not have had a brain injury, or to have lost my ability to speak, or breathe on my own. There were others around me in worse shape: I used this knowledge to look at my own proverbial cup as half full rather than half empty.

Then, after a month, I was able to move my right shoulder ever so slightly. I tried so hard to make this happen. Every day as I lay in my hospital bed it seemed that I was doing isometric shoulder shrugs, like pushing against a solid surface above my shoulder. Then, poof — my right shoulder moved. So this is what everyone was waiting for? Why were they so excited about a shrug? What could that do for me? But then, a few days later, I was able to move my arm a little. Well, actually, it was a minute movement of my forearm! Still not enough to be functional, but movement there was. This meant that the doctors were wrong. I WOULD be able to move something below my neck. And this was just the beginning.... I now had something to strengthen — and possibly to use!

After three months, I had some movement in my right wrist. Now I began to be hopeful! As movement moved down my right arm, I had something more to strengthen. I had a *purpose* for the exercises. I might actually be able *to work my arm*....

After five months, struggling with my weak shoulder and arm muscles and using a bent spoon placed into the pocket of my leather hand splint, I finally got my arm up high enough to attempt to feed myself. Oh my God! I could do something for myself! Although I was finally able to lift a spoon of mashed potatoes, or anything solid, it took me two more *years* to have a steady enough arm to lift a spoon of soup. We celebrated the day I first got those potatoes in my mouth as if I had just run my first marathon! It didn't even matter that it landed in my lap as many times as it did in my mouth. A simple, taken-for-granted task I did without thought before my accident was now a task that took monumental effort for me.

Before becoming paralyzed, I used to plan an activity every year around my birthday. The activity was always something that would push me to a new limit. On my 28th birthday, I rode my bike to the beach, around the Bay, and back — 25 miles in all. The year of my accident I was planning on hiking down to the bottom of the Grand Canyon and/or going white water rafting. Now I was fighting daily for even the smallest movements and improvements.

However, little by little, day by day, after almost a year of con-centrated effort, I learned to write again. To do that, I had to train the large muscles in my shoulder to handle the fine motor coordina-tion necessary for my arm to form the small letters I had become accustomed to doing before my accident. Now, however, my alpha-bet looked like that of a kindergartner learning to write. It was painstakingly slow and very shaky. Each letter was about one-inch tall. It took another year to get my alphabet to the average height of personal correspondence. It was three years before I could turn *that* into cursive. It was always challenging, and sometimes discourag-ing, but I had something tangible to look at each time I tried to write. Vain as it is, it has always been difficult for me to compare my new writing to my old, attractive handwriting of which I had always been so proud. We did not have computers then; everything was written by hand. My handwriting was part of my identity.

It has been over 30 years now, and I am still learning what my body can do — and often, what it's trying to tell me (more on that later). I have a different perspective at this time in my journey. Upon reflection I can see the interwoven themes of my life merging in this timeline of events. My accident had paralyzed not only my body, but in many ways my mind and spirit as well.

I will probably mention more than once that I am something of a Pollyanna, who even when things are bad, sees a light at the end of the tunnel. I have always seen this light as a gift from God drawing me out the other end. But as you will read in the next two chapters, years would pass for me to be able to pull myself through to the "other side" — to *The Up Side of Down.*

Throughout the years, I have hit walls and had breakthroughs. I find the following poem, *Courage Doesn't Always Roar*, to be especially meaningful, as I too, have always had that quiet voice that says, "Tomorrow I'll try again."

What really catches my attention in this poem is the idea that I do not need to be defined by my circumstances. The choice to go beyond my paralysis and decide how I will respond to my life is all up to me. Recognizing this *choice* is one of the themes repeated throughout the book. And *choosing life*, with God's help, is a decision I continue to make every day.

COURAGE DOESN'T ALWAYS ROAR

By Paula Fox

When you run out of strength
and you want to give up
because it's too much to bear...

I want to remind you, my precious friend,
that you have what it takes inside...
extraordinary courage that may not ROAR,
but it doesn't cower and hide.

It's the quiet voice inside you that says,
"Tomorrow I'll try again."
It's the courage to keep on going...
to see things through to the end.

You are not defined by this moment in time.
You are not what has happened to you;
It's the way you choose to respond that matters
and what you decide to do.

Courage is not the absence of fear,
but a powerful choice we make...
the choice to move forward with PURPOSE
...regardless of what it takes.

It's the courage that's found in ordinary women
who are HEROES in their own way,
exhibiting strength and fortitude
in life's challenges every day...

Valiant woman of exceptional courage
with enduring power to cope...
taking each problem one day at a time
and never giving up HOPE.

We're encouraged by the faith of others
to survive and overcome,
with the courage to say, "I may be down...
but the battle is not done!"

For the WOMAN of COURAGE is a winner...
regardless of what she loses;
She displays amazing beauty and strength
with the attitude she chooses.

She gives herself the permission she needs...
to feel disappointed or sad.
But then she empowers herself with faith...
to focus on good things...not bad

Her story is one of gentle strength
reminding us all once more...
Steel is sometimes covered in velvet
and...

Courage doesn't always roar.

ENDINGS AND BEGINNINGS

A divorce is like an amputation: you survive it,
but there's less of you.

— Margaret Atwood

I went back to work very soon — only eight months after such a horrific accident. I *needed* to be there as it felt like my only lifeline to my old self. Yet even though I was back at work and moving on with my life as a teacher, over the next few years other parts of my life were spiraling downhill. I must have been in denial of, or oblivious to, how bad some things had gotten, because I did not see my next challenge coming.

Four years after my accident, I decided to start counseling. As my husband drove me to my first counseling session, he told me he wanted a divorce. *What?* I could barely breathe — I was being abandoned by the person I most relied on, my rock! Could I survive being rejected by the person I loved the most? I felt totally alone. Although I knew that 95% of marriages don't survive this type of dramatic event, I thought if any man could make it, Mike could. What now? How much worse could my life get?

When I realized that Mike could no longer cope with my new reality and that my marriage was no different from all those other statistics, I was devastated! We had gone through a rough patch a few years earlier, but I thought we had come out the other side stronger. I really loved him and felt that was reciprocal. *The pain of my divorce felt far worse than that of breaking my neck.*

As I look back on this time now, I can better understand the stress Mike must've been under. I was a different person then. Because of spasms and phantom pains, I left Rehab addicted to Valium, which is very mind-altering. (Later with the help of my physician and acupuncture, I weaned myself off the drug.) During these first four "post-injury" years, I was dependent on Mike for everything — in addition to his full-time job, he was my counselor, chauffeur, phone holder, nose scratcher, and part-time caregiver (to name just a few.) It was too much for anyone to handle. We went to couples counseling as well as seeing separate therapists. When it came down to the final wire, I knew I had to let him go. I didn't want him staying with me unless he wanted to be with me. What is that famous quote: "If you love someone, set them free; if they come back, it was meant to be." (Source unknown.) There is a lot of wisdom in those words.

Looking back, I have many regrets about this time in my life; but there were so many lessons I had to learn. Some lessons we have to learn over and over, yet others we may not realize we've learned until years later. Perhaps the one positive outcome of my divorce is that my not having Mike to lean on may have helped me find my way back to independence faster than if I'd stayed married. I had no other choice!

I know God will not give me anything I can't handle.
I just wish that He didn't trust me so much.

— Mother Teresa

—⟊⟊⟊—

I had an incredibly difficult several years after my divorce. As one can imagine, I was extremely fragile during this time. I was suicidal and looking for reasons to keep on living, and television programming and the Hollywood film industry did not help.

When I broke my neck in 1978, both a movie and the TV series, *Dallas*, came out about quads and death. On *Dallas,* my Friday night favorite, they pulled the plug to spare a quad from this *awful fate.* The movie, *Whose Life is It, Anyway*? with Richard Dreyfus, was about the right to die with dignity. Both of these shows, and others, conveyed the same misleading message — life was not worth living for a quadriplegic!

I also realized during this time that death takes many forms. For me it was the death of my marriage, the death of the future I had planned, and the loss of the children I had hoped to have. I was miserable and not at all sure of *why I was living.*

One time I was so depressed I remember sitting in my bedroom in front of my dresser looking at myself in the mirror. I couldn't move. I was paralyzed, not by my body, but by my depression. It had me stuck in one place — physically and emotionally.

This moment is still vivid to me because, as I look back on it now, I know I had an "out-of-body experience" that day. I was floating near the ceiling looking down at myself in front of my dresser, in that stuck place. I've often wondered about that experience. I think that my "real self" had to leave my body in order to leave the pain — much like people with multiple personalities develop a new personality to help them function in a painful situation. I relive that experience over and over each time I hear other people speak of similar experiences.

It is a good thing I was in counseling. It took almost five years of seeing a psychologist before I felt that my life was back on track and I could move forward.

I found the poem on the next page during this time when I was having so many feelings of loss. It is often difficult for me to put my feelings into words, but this poem helped me understand myself better, and let me know that others have experienced the same emotions.

Each experience that ends well helps me the next time a seemingly negative change occurs. Deliberately choosing *life* over *death* has not always been easy: in fact, at times it has been extremely difficult.

ENDINGS

By Robin Williams

Endings are so hard for me, God.
They don't seem as painful for other people,
But everything within me cries out for sameness,
Continuity, Familiarity.

New beginnings are scary for me to even consider
Far away they are exciting,
But up close, new beginnings terrify me.

Tonight I am hating the responsibility
Of "yes and no" decisions that I am facing.

Maybe my idealism simply can't handle
Clear-eyed reality.
That is why I can't stand realistic movie endings
that leave me sad,
Despondent, angry.

I want to be able to gaze clear-eyed,
I want to be objective, level with perspective.

Yet I hate the pain of ending a dream,
A relationship, a good book
A lovely evening with someone.

There is a deep sigh that escapes
from the depths of me
when I consider a new home,
A new set of people, new values,
New lifestyles, new goals.
I ache to stay with what is familiar.
Mostly, I ache to stay with what is secure.
I struggle to weigh endings and beginnings, God.
But, paradoxically, I can't live without them.

Crises, change, endings, beginnings....
They are my source of life, direction, hope.

My accident had forced a profound end to my life as I had known it. Now I was not only having to cope with changes such as a new job, new friends, a new home, or a new city. I now had to make a complete paradigm shift in my thinking and begin a new life as a single woman.

Hope during this time was the little ray of light I always saw at the other end of a long, black tunnel. But no matter how long and how black the tunnel was, there was always a light — God's light. Always, it gave me some purpose for moving forward or a direction to turn. It was like a little push of fresh air, gently indicating how I was to shift, or where I was to fix my gaze. I started looking for a reason to go on living, to begin living a completely different life. Maybe that's what the light is — a reason to go on living.

Somewhere along the way I decided a good reason for being alive was to become what God intended me to be! This realization gave me the hope, the impetus, and the motivation to begin my life anew. First, however, I had to pray about discerning what God had in mind for me.

Where was I to find the answer to that? I knew I was a Child of God; I could feel His presence in my life. But there was the ever-present question — what *is* His purpose for me? The answer to this question did not come all at once, but in time, come it did....

VICTIM OR VICTOR

I can be changed by what happens to me,
but I refuse to be reduced by it.

— Maya Angelou

I had real problems with my self-image after my accident. I hated my body. In the beginning I would use a solid board as a lap tray so that I wouldn't even have to see the bottom half of my body. I never felt like I had anything below the waist anyway because, as a quadriplegic, I could not feel or use any of my lower half or extremities. I pictured my body like a hunk of Swiss cheese with the holes in it representing all that I could no longer do. Sometimes I felt as if I were just a "head on a box" — like a show I had seen on *Star Trek*. I was thankful that I had no brain injury and could still use my head for understanding what was going on and learning to manage my life, but most days that was not enough for me.

So, four years after my injury, I decided to start counseling. This was my first step toward moving from a space of self-hatred, discouragement, and despair to one of acceptance of my body and who I was at this point in my life. It wasn't as easy as that sounds, however. I might have started counseling because of my body issues, but I soon learned that they were only the tip of the iceberg. This was the agenda I started with — but now with Mike saying he wanted a divorce — all else was preempted. The issue first and foremost on my mind became, "How do I get through this pain, and how do I live my life as a single woman?"

As I worked through my divorce and other issues, I realized that the most important lesson I was learning from counseling was to recognize when I was falling into a *Victim* role, and how I could turn that around to be the *Victor* of the situation.

Every week I was showing up at my session with another sad story of all that had happened to me during the week. There was always something to complain about or cry about (a bladder infection, a broken wheelchair, another bad caregiver). Every week was worse, and my life felt like it was spinning out of control. It was so much easier to make excuses and wallow in self-pity than to take responsibility for my life. After all, "*I*" couldn't help it if my electric bed broke or my caregiver did not show up. I was a victim — a victim of all my circumstances and surroundings. I had all the classic symptoms:

- **I felt cheated and blamed others** for all that was happening to me.

- **I felt sorry for myself**: "Why is it always me?"

- **I saw only problems**, and I played them up for maximum attention and to give myself reasons for seeking sympathy and being depressed.

From Viktor Frankl's book, *Man's Search for Meaning*, I learned that "self-pity imprisons us in the walls of our own self-absorption." He goes on to explain that the whole world shrinks down to the size of our problem, and the more we dwell on it, the smaller we are and the larger the problem seems to grow.

Yes, I had shrunk the whole world down to the realm of my never-ending problems. I dwelt on them; I wallowed in them. Nothing else seemed to matter. I noticed no beauty or good in my life; I heard no birds singing; I saw no sunsets. My problems were my whole world. This was the paralysis of mind and spirit that the accident had brought in its wake; feeling sorry for myself consumed my whole existence. My world was small, indeed; and there was no room to recognize (let alone appreciate) the good around me. I was not seeing the proverbial "light at the end of the tunnel" at this time.

Now, because my marriage had ended, I felt that I was *really* by myself. My next tangible lesson in the "victim/victor school of life" involved finding and keeping good caregivers. This is always a challenge for people with severe disabilities. Now it became my first priority. And wouldn't you know, the very first night that I was to be on my own after my husband left, I had a new attendant. She was trained and this was her first night to get me ready for the night, transfer me out of the wheelchair and into bed. She would then stay there until my morning attendant came. THAT NEVER HAPPENED! She called me from jail to say that she had been arrested and would not be able to work with me. Panic set in. What now? I was again instantly a victim with no Plan B to fall back on. (That was almost 30 years ago and even as big and important as it was then, for the life of me, I cannot remember her name or how I got to bed that night!)

Dr. Kris Laverty, the psychologist I was seeing, saw through it all. In time, she taught me to recognize the *victim* in me — and to catch myself before falling into that role again. What was the alternative? To become a *victor*, of course! Even today I am still learning to stay in the victor role and take responsibility for myself and my actions. I follow this advice:

- **Don't blame others** for my situation and don't make excuses.

- **Determine what I need**, where to get it, from whom it is available, and how to ask for it.

- **Learn how to take confident steps** toward solving my problems.

As a result of my experience that night without a caregiver (and many other events that followed), I slowly learned how to take positive control of my life. I had allowed myself to feel victimized. I realized that I could free myself from much of my anguish with a change in perspective and attitude and, therefore, transform myself from victim to victor. I did not have to live in panic mode. No longer the same person in my thinking and actions, I slowly began to:

- **Think proactively**. For instance, drinking enough water (and maybe cranberry juice) can help prevent bladder infections. Also, learning to "read" my body can help me seek medical treatment before the symptoms are serious.

- **Always have a Plan B....** And C.... And D.... With backup plans in place, I am almost never left stranded.

- **Polish communication skills.** I sharpened my interviewing skills (for caregivers), learned how to ask better questions and to become a better listener.

Wishing, waiting, and hoping —
that's the language of victims.
Those are all passive words. They're not active.
If you want things to happen in your life,
you have to get moving —
even if it's just one small step.

— Cathy Conheim

Once I crawled out from under my rock of depression, I was able to predict and/or prepare for my most common stumbling blocks. I could stop being a victim of fate or circumstance and become empowered to manage my life. I felt as though life no longer "just happened" to me without my having some say in the matter, I could take some degree of control.

I don't want to understate the difficulty of learning this lesson — or the struggle of therapy as a whole. I saw Dr. Laverty for several years. Over time, my sessions went from once or twice a week to once a month. They were difficult, and I hated it every time she said to me, "You have to move *through* the pain — there's no way *around* it." Oftentimes, the hour would be up, and the session would end before I felt ready. I would still have a gnawing pain in the pit of my stomach and think to myself, "but I can't wait until the next session...." (In this situation, journaling helped.) Therapy takes time. Grieving takes time. I'm fortunate — blessed, actually — that I had so many people to help me through it.

The quotes that I have included on the next page have helped me affirm the steps I've taken and the choices I've made. Affirmation is a powerfully good thing, and I believe these affirmations helped me create my new reality.

Life is not about waiting for the storm to pass...
It's about learning to dance in the rain.

— Vivian Greene

Life at any time can become difficult:
life at any time can become easy.
It all depends upon how one adjusts oneself to life.

— Morarji Desai, Prime Minister of India

Though no one can go back and make a brand new start,
anyone can start from now and make a brand new ending.

— Carl Bard

FIRST, LIKE YOURSELF

Self-Acceptance

Success is liking yourself, liking what you do,
and liking how you do it.

— Maya Angelou

Throughout the next several years, issues of accepting my body — and my whole "self" — came up often. There were many lessons to learn; one that related to self-image unexpectedly "hit me upside the head" when I was attending a class for my Master's Degree in Education.

I was teaching during the day and was often tired when attending night classes. It was always a treat when we had guest speakers, and this particular evening our guest was speaking about disabilities. My first thought was that I could have skipped this particular class, but I was soon engaged in the personal stories of a "little person." I was surprised by the similarity of our experiences, even though our disabilities were so very different. In talking about her social circles, friendships and work, she said that she deliberately chose not to have very many friends who were "little." She told us that when she looked at someone of normal height, she felt that she, too, was normal height.

I realized I had been doing the same thing. The first thing I thought of was how often my girlfriends were thin — something I only aspired to be. But when I looked at them, I, too, felt thin. Thinking as far back as high school — a lifetime ago, I was not particularly popular, but I had popular friends. I think that somehow made me feel I was part of that crowd, also.

That night in class, I realized the very obvious: I did not have many friends in wheelchairs! I was often able to forget that I was in the chair when all those around me were able-bodied. I was surrounding myself with other people who looked the way I wanted to look. In fact, I recall the first time I visited the rehab center, and everyone was in a wheelchair. I remember thinking, "I'm not like them." But I was; I just wasn't ready to accept it yet.

Most importantly, I think, is that since I did not see myself as disabled, I thought I would someday free myself psychologically from my wheelchair and go on to accomplish things despite my disability. Looking back at how I felt then, I learned that I could both accept my disability *and* move on to an accomplished life. I would not allow myself to be defined by my wheelchair or my paralysis.

After I recognized what I'd been doing, I wandered outside my comfort zone and joined groups and attended meetings of people with disabilities. I became a guest speaker, representing "the disabled." By doing this, I opened myself up to new experiences and friendships that I would never have had. I did not want to be in denial. I did, however, make a conscious decision that I wanted to *work* among able-bodied people rather than in a community of people with disabilities; for example, a convalescent home, a hospital, or with a medical supply company. I'm sure I could have had a good career in either group, but I enjoyed my place out in the world where I could teach students that "being disabled" does not mean "being unable."

The quotation below seems to encompass what I learned from that graduate class so long ago. Recognizing my discomfort propelled me into a new and much better reality.

The truth is that our finest moments are most likely to occur when we are feeling deeply uncomfortable, unhappy, or unfulfilled.

For it is only in such moments, propelled by our discomfort, that we are likely to step out of our ruts and start searching for different ways or truer answers.

— M. Scott Peck

FAITH

I have called you by your name; you are mine

— Isaiah 43:1

God has called me by name; I am His.

Although I received my first Bible for Easter from my German grandmother when I was in third grade — how I treasured that little white Bible! I was not raised in church. My mom was a non-observant Jew, and my dad was not interested in church or religion. From childhood through high school, I went to Sunday School and church with friends. Then, in my freshman year of college, I was handed a newspaper entitled *Revolution* (published by Campus Crusade for Christ), and my new life began…. I realized God had been calling me — by name — since I was about 10 years old.

Someone from a Campus Crusade meeting shared this verse with me.

I stand at the door and knock;
if anyone hears my voice and opens the door,
I will come in and sup with him and he with me.

— Revelation 3:20

I knew God was talking to me and I prayed that night that He would come into my heart and into my life. I am embarrassed to say that I really did not have much confidence in my prayer, so I asked God to show me some silly, yet tangible proof (like having a closed window open on its own) that He had heard me. It was irrational and absurd, but I needed it, and God knew it. I woke up feeling like a completely new person. And the proof that I asked for? It's hard to explain in words. I had been having a very difficult time with my mother, as many 18-year-olds do. In fact, I was thankful for the 500 miles between us. But when I woke up that next morning, I felt an overwhelming love for her and felt compelled to call her and tell her so. For me, at that time, it was miraculous and all the proof I needed. That was February 1968. I know that not everyone has the "born again" experience as strongly as I did, but once you've experienced hearing God answer, it's hard to ever doubt Him again.

I was baptized that summer. I participated in Bible studies, joined a church, married a Christian man, and led my sister to Christ. I loved my life. I do remember, however, as a new Christian, two conscious prayers:

- Please don't send me to Africa as a missionary.

- After reading Joni Eareckson Tada's book (the true story of a girl who broke her neck the summer after high school and then used her recovery time to grow closer to God), I never wanted to be apart from God to the point that I would need to *become paralyzed* in order to find my way back. Wow, it is hard to believe that I actually prayed that prayer!

Then, not many years later — my accident! It surprises many people when I tell them that I never got angry, questioned God or asked, "Why me?" A popular book of that era was Elisabeth Kubler-Ross' *On Death and Dying*, in which she outlines Seven Stages of Grief. Being angry with God is one of the stages in the process. As much as I was told that identifying these steps in my own grieving process would help me, they never seemed to apply. Although I didn't always recognize it, I knew that God had been holding me in the palm of His hands. I had had many sad and lonely times, but I blamed them on my circumstances — not on God. I'm not sure why, but I never felt a need to reconcile the two. The piece below speaks to the love and trust I felt toward God before my accident, and it held me up through those *dark times*.

NEVER DOUBT IN THE DARKNESS WHAT YOU ONCE BELIEVED IN THE LIGHT

When hardship settles in, dark and brooding emotions can surge over us in a tide of doubt and fear.

The only sure dike against a flood of glum feelings is to remember.

We must recall sunnier times when we drove the pilings of God's goodness deep in our hearts.

Happier times when we felt our moorings of trust hold ground.

When we lived on His blessings, knew His favor, were grateful for His gifts, and felt the flesh and blood of His everlasting arms underneath us.

— Source Unknown

—⟨ɷ⟩—

I feel certain that it takes us a lifetime to have a complete understanding of our faith and to fully develop what we believe to be true. Things are not black and white for me, and I am becoming more and more comfortable with the shades of gray. I am also more peaceful with the many mysteries that my faith presents, and I trust that God has many more secrets to reveal to me in His time and when He believes I am ready.

—⟨ɷ⟩—

Faith for me does not merely mean believing in the being, goodness, and power of God, but trusting in the truths and promises of His Word and all that He said would come to pass.

Of particular assurance to me in this paralyzed body of mine is my faith in the promises of heaven. I am not afraid of dying because I know that death is not the end of life — only the end of life as we know it on Earth. I believe that my spirit will leave this broken body and be given a new, healthy body. I will dance again.

He will wipe every tear from their eyes.
There will be no more death or mourning or crying or pain…
"I am making everything new!"
                                          — Revelation 21: 4-5

... When we die and leave these bodies, we will have...
an eternal body made for us by God himself....
We grow weary in our present bodies,
and we long for the day when we will put on
our heavenly bodies
like new clothing.... We want to slip into our new bodies....
— 2 Corinthians 5:1-4

Another important aspect of my faith is my belief in prayer. The Bible instructs us to make our prayers definite and specific; mine are, therefore, unmistakable requests for the things I want. I believe God listens and answers my prayers in His time and in His way. I have faith that His ways are good and right beyond anything I might expect or could ever imagine. I also know that I might not receive an answer when I want, or that I might not receive an answer that is recognizable in relation to the original prayer. That's okay with me now. I have seen so many prayers answered that I have faith in the process.

Therefore I say to you,
all things for which you pray and ask,
believe that you have received them,
and they will be granted you.
— Mark 11:24

Prayer is the verbal release of faith —
a specific faith for a specific purpose,
all based on a specific promise from God.

— paraphrased from Joni Eareckson Tada,
Pearls of Great Price

Do not be anxious about anything, but in everything,
by prayer and petition, with thanksgiving,
present your requests to God.

— *Philippians 4:6*

━∽∾∽━

I know that God loves me and is always with me, and I find it sad how often I need His gentle (and sometimes not so gentle) reminders. Although I knew that Dr. Laverty was a Christian, I was not consciously thinking about God during my counseling sessions. Yet an odd thing happened at the end of each session. I would drive down by the ocean and sit and journal both about what I had discussed and what had been Dr. Laverty's response. If I did not do this, I almost always forgot everything from the session by the time I got home. (I later learned that "forgetting" was a defense mechanism against reliving the painful memories that had been dredged up during the sessions.) I usually wrote for about 20 to 30 minutes, and as I finished the entry into my notebook, I always ended up with *Amen.* I did not do this on purpose, but it happened week after week and I came to realize that it was a truth I KNEW in my heart; it was God's way of telling me that He was there with me going through these painful times. I have since learned to recognize more and more ways that God reminds me that He is with me. Whether by an unexpected Amen after journaling, by waking up in the middle of the night with solutions to questions or problems, or by remembering an incident or appointment that I would never have thought of on my own, I am the grateful recipient of reminders of His everlasting presence within me.

⁓∾⁓

One of the greatest lessons my faith has taught me is that of forgiveness. I have had my share of disappointments in the actions of others. Family, friends, employers, and — fill in the blank — all did things at some point in time which hurt and saddened me. Small transgressions are easy to overlook and forgive, but the big things are so much harder. As I have mentioned earlier, the saddest event to happen in my life was my husband leaving. The pain in my heart was as real and physical as it was emotional and mental. I lived with the burden of disappointment in him for years.

Then one day I felt compelled (I believe urged by God) to forgive him. I prayed a very simple prayer humbly asking for God's help to rid my heart of the sorrow, grief, and general unhappiness I was feeling. I also asked God to help me to forgive Mike for leaving me. The experience was so "life-changing" that it is still vivid in my memory. In fact, I still remember exactly where I was sitting. I remained there quietly for a few minutes after praying; then, in what I can only consider a miracle, I had a very physical response. My shoulders relaxed as the weight dissipated, the knot in my stomach and the pain in my heart disappeared in an instant. I felt light and unencumbered! The sensation I felt was as huge and unexpected as when I first had invited God into my life. Again, I believe that once anyone has experienced God's miracles, he or she will never forget them. One experiences an interior knowing with total certainty. I am not saying here that the sadness of my divorce went away in an instant. It still saddens me today, but the hurt, pain, and weight of it left me. The negative feelings and the accompanying heaviness I had felt toward Mike left me, and I was free to remember the good times.

———◦∞◦———

There are many verses from the Bible that are particularly important to me. There are two that I would like to share. This first one is:

In all thy ways acknowledge Him
and He shall direct thy paths.

— Proverbs 3:5, 6

And the other:

This is the day the Lord has made,
let us rejoice and be glad in it.

— Psalms 118:24

The verse above is one of my favorites, and below is a paraphrased meditation I found based on it that expresses my own feelings so well.

Every day that we are given is a precious gift from God. We should wake up every morning with a grateful attitude, full of faith and expectancy for what the Lord has in store. Sure, you may be facing some challenges in your everyday life, or maybe things aren't going the way you planned; but remember, each new day is a chance to stand strong in the midst of adversity and see the faithfulness of God. Every new day is an opportunity to praise and thank Him; to magnify your God instead of magnifying your problems.

This is the day that the Lord has made, let us rejoice and be glad in it! Be glad that God has promised never to leave us or forsake us. Be glad that God has given you a sound, healthy mind. Rejoice that He is making a way where there seems to be no way! As you focus on the gift of every day and rejoice in what God has done in your life, you will begin to experience His increase and blessings. You'll rise up higher and set the course to live in victory all the days of your life!

How beautiful this is! I use Bible verses as affirmations of all the good that God brings me. I have this verse pasted on the dashboard of my car as a reminder to delight in the day.

GRACE

Grace — such a "religious" sounding word. What does it really mean? Grace simply means favor, mercy, or blessing.

What does it mean to me? To me, Grace isn't simple at all. In my life Grace is miraculous. Have you ever accomplished anything so overwhelming that you knew you must be running on super-power? God's Grace is like that for me, and I have never felt it as strongly as this past year.

Pressure sores are my *Achilles' heel*. By sitting in a wheelchair for an average of 15 hours a day over the past 30+ years, I continually damaged my skin. I know I don't do "pressure relief" often enough, but it's difficult to recline every hour while teaching a class of 35 high school students (excuses, excuses). Throughout the years, I have fought several lengthy battles with pressure sores which land me in bed for months at a time. It's frustrating to be stuck in bed, I feel more disabled than usual. Without gravity to help me, I can only move my head and right arm so I'm unable to write, feed myself, or do anything productive.

The year 2011 was terrible. I had surgery to close a long-standing pressure sore. For my recuperation, I expected to be in bed for six weeks. When six weeks became three months, I realized I would have to retire. I had been teaching 39 years, and this decision was not an easy one to make, but I saw that I would not be able to return to a full-time teaching job. Three months became six months, and before I knew it I had been in bed for over a year. Good thing we can't see into the future; I never would have believed I could make it.

People ask me, "How have you managed to remain so upbeat?" or "What's it like to be in bed so long?" Actually, I'm just as amazed as others. I know this year hasn't been about my strength; it was about God's strength. He is the only reason I have not fallen into a miserable depression. I know I am not strong enough, or a positive enough thinker, to have done it myself.

Surrounded by God's Grace, I was not allowed to become a victim of my bed. I hardly ever get bored, and this time was no different. I found interesting things to do while lying flat on my back. A friend bought me a new laptop and with the help of a microphone and dictation software, others created a way for me to use it while lying on my back. In fact, I used this incredible gift to write this book, something I promised myself I would do when I retired. In addition, I listened to a new book on tape every week; I was visited by many friends and family and did lots of spiritual soul-searching to see what I could learn from this time of quiet. The following poem has been a beautiful reminder to me during several of my long recuperation periods that, although I may not like it at the time, God can use all of my circumstances for good. Of course, I had a few days of tears and a few days of boredom, but for the most part — "No prison, my bed!"

I Needed the Quiet

By Alice H. Mortenson

I needed the quiet, so He drew me aside
Into the shadows, where we could confide
Away from the hustle, where all the day long
I hurried and worried, when active and strong,

I needed the quiet, tho at first I rebelled
But gently so gently my cross He upheld
And whispered so sweetly of spiritual things;
Tho weakened in body, my spirit took wings
To heights never dreamed of when active all day.
He loved me so greatly, He drew me away.

I needed the quiet, no prison my bed
But a beautiful valley of blessings instead
A place to grow richer, in Jesus to hide;
I needed the quiet, so He drew me aside.

TAKING RESPONSIBILITY

Search for Life's Meaning

*I am confident that each of us is responsible
for creating a meaningful life
for ourselves and for what we can do for others.*

— Paulo Coelho

After my accident, as is obvious, I suffered huge losses in my ability to do most things. I could no longer lace up tennis shoes and jog, play tennis, or hike. I could no longer feel the fresh, cool water in a pool or at the beach. Never again would I feel the ivory keys of a piano, move fabric through a sewing machine, or feel the dirt move through my fingers as I planted a rose bush. We are so often defined by what we can do (teacher, piano player, artist, and so on) so when I lost my ability to "do" things, I also lost "me." I felt like that hunk of Swiss cheese whose holes represent all the things I could no longer do.

It was important for me to hang on to the two things I thought I could still be — a teacher and a wife (and being a wife was *iffy* even at the beginning.) Who was I? What else could I do or be? I went back to teaching high school only eight months after breaking my neck. I had to! I needed some identity.

During that time of deep depression, I felt like I needed to reinvent myself, so I did a lot of reading, searching for identity, a feeling of self, and "the meaning of life." Viktor Frankl, a survivor of the Nazi prison camps, observed the various ways in which men and women responded to suffering, and in his book, *Man's Search for Meaning*, he wrote:

> In the final analysis it becomes clear that the sort of person we become is the result of an inner decision, not the result of the suffering alone.

> That life ultimately means taking the responsibility to find the right answer to its problems....

This was a huge lesson for me. I kept looking for something external to happen, to bring my life meaning, or to make my life meaningful. Here, again, I learned that ultimately the choice was mine — and I chose Life....

Although the world is full of suffering,
it is also full of the
overcoming of it.

— Helen Keller

The most authentic thing about us is our capacity to create, to
overcome, to endure, to transform, to love
and to be greater than our suffering.

— Ben Okri

Everything can be taken from a man but one thing:
the last of the human freedoms—
to choose one's attitude in any given set of circumstances,
to choose one's own way.

— Victor Frankl

The willingness to accept responsibility for one's own life
is the source from which self-respect springs.

— Joan Didion

LIFE CYCLES

Death, Hope, and Resurrection

Life is a celebration of awakenings, of new beginnings,
and of wonderful surprises that enlighten the soul.

— *Cielo*

Accepting change, letting go, having hope, and trusting that new life will come is a lesson that I learned not only from books like Victor Frankl's, but also from another of my friends and mentors, the Rev. Patricia Moore. She helped me understand that life is full of transitions, a cycle of change that frequently involves death, hope, resurrection — and new life.

Pat spent time with me during the Easter season. She explained that in the words of the church the whole cycle would be known as:

Life — Letting go — Death — Tomb —
Hope — Resurrection — New Life

Not only did I understand the Lenten season, Holy Week and Easter in a much deeper way after speaking with Pat, but I also began seeing many of these cycles appearing throughout my own experiences.

Here's an example. Before my accident I had a wonderful job as a teacher and an ASB (activities) Advisor at a high school here in San Diego. I enjoyed the students, the school events, my colleagues — all of it. *Life*. After seven years my life had changed. Not only was I now in a wheelchair, but the politics of the school were also different. I knew things would never be the same. *Letting go*. Things got worse and I knew I needed to leave. *Death*. While in the *Tomb*, I thought about what I needed: To look for a new position. *Hope*. Another rewarding job at a different school became available, plus I had had time for personal growth and renewal. *Resurrection*. After realizing all the benefits of my move, I began to recognize that I had a *New Life*.

It sounds simplistic, but once I began to see this cycle running through my life, it became easier to again trust God that He was alive and well in my life, and that good things would come.

> *And we know that in all things God works for the good*
> *for those who love Him,*
> *who have been called according to His purpose.*
>
> — *Romans* 8:28

Another example involved my caregiver — this is the person who takes care of my most basic needs on a daily basis, and nothing occurs in my life without a good person in this position. I found my first really good live-in attendant after several disastrous situations. My life — my home and my health — was finally running smoothly. It was the best it had been for the past six years. *Life*. Then Miki, my attendant, decided to get married and move away. *Letting go*. My tranquility, as I'd known it, was about to leave. *Death*. There was quite a while with no regular attendant and no one good in sight. *Tomb.* As any victor would (and I did by that time see myself as a victor, not a victim), I started working new possibilities. I even took Spanish lessons to brush up on my now rusty skills, which I had learned a decade earlier in high school Spanish class. Being this close to the Mexican border meant that one of my most logical selections for a caregiver might be a Hispanic woman. *Hope.* I was right! Enter Lupe — and things were better beyond hope and belief. *Resurrection* and *New Life.* That was 28 years ago, and she is still with me!

I recognized the cycle during this past year-and-a-half when going from *Life*, to learning that I would have surgery, *Letting Go*, to my time in bed — *Death* and *Tomb* — to thinking about using my time constructively, *Hope*, and ultimately to finishing my book — *Resurrection* and *New Life.*

I was once again reassured that even through the worst and most tragic of circumstances, events, and disappointments, there is the promise of *New Life*…. Every experience that ends with *New Life* increases one's ability to trust that the next cycle will also end well. Even though my examples of life cycles lasted for months, I have also experienced this entire cycle in a matter of a day — or even an hour.

> *Rise from your fears and go out into the sunlight*
> *to meet Me, your Risen Lord.*
> *Each day will have much in it that you will meet either*
> *in the spirit of the tomb, or in the spirit of Resurrection.*
> *Deliberately choose the one and reject the other.*
>
> — from *God Calling*

BUILDING A MEANINGFUL LIFE

Searching for Purpose

The purpose of life is a life of purpose.

— Robert Byrne

Why are we here? What is our purpose?

I could not express it any better than did Cherie Carter-Scott, Ph.D. in her book, *If Life Is a Game… These Are the Rules.*

> Each of us has his or her own purpose for being here. It is unique and separate from anyone else's. It is a journey, and once we discover this "mystery of purpose" we can actually begin living it. When we are working toward fulfilling our true purpose, we discover astonishing gifts within ourselves that we may have never known we have.

At first my search for life's purpose was more about trying to live a "normal" life within an "abnormal" body, and showing others that I could still be productive and able to give back to society. Later, I saw helping others as one of my reasons for being here. Service has always given me a sense of fulfillment and satisfaction.

Nick Vujic, who was born without limbs, travels around the world as a motivational speaker encouraging others to find their purpose. He said that he finally figured out through his experiences that the hardships we people with disabilities face provide us with even greater opportunities to discover who we are meant to be and how we can share our gifts to benefit others.

I spent a lot of time praying about God's plan for my life. I knew I could begin by identifying and focusing on the gifts God has given me — applying them, sharing them, and taking joy in using them.

> *Our talent is God's gift to us and what we do with it is our gift back to God.*
>
> — Leo Buscaglia

We all have gifts and talents to share. I have been blessed with good leadership and organizational skills, and I've used them to help enable others to work effectively and reach their goals. One example of this occurred when an arsonist with schizophrenia burned down the sanctuary at my church. While some parishioners ministered to him in prison and others prepared our fellowship hall to double as the sanctuary, I felt led to help raise money to rebuild. I worked with a group of us to begin the new Congregational Development Plan, the "Do the Dream" campaign. I also used these skills at my school when I wrote and received a grant that named only a few schools in the country with a special status as an *Academy of Information Technology*. This grant funded several new programs and a computer lab for my school.

I know that another of my gifts is that of optimism. I have seen how it helps me personally, especially getting through the hard times. However, I am just beginning to see how being optimistic can help me in assisting or serving others.

In his book, *Learned Optimism: How to Change Your Mind and Your Life*, Martin Seligman "points to optimism not only as a means to individual well-being, but also as a powerful aid in finding your purpose and contributing to the world." (As written in an article by Maria Popova of Brain Pickings.)

> *Optimism is invaluable for the meaningful life.*
> *With a firm belief in a positive future*
> *you can throw yourself into the service*
> *of that which is larger than you are.*
>
> — **Martin Seligman**

I think we all want to leave this world a better place. Combining that desire with something that brings me true joy is like adding soft, sweet marshmallows to my hot chocolate.

Our souls are hungry for meaning,
for the sense that we have figured out how to live
so that our lives matter,
so that the world will be at least a little bit different
for our having passed through it...
What frustrates us and robs our lives of joy
is this absence of meaning...
Does our being alive matter?

— Harold S. Kushner

When you love people and have the desire
to make a profound, positive impact upon the world,
then will you have accomplished the meaning to life.

— Sasha Azevedo

SERVICE

...I am only one, but I am one.
I can't do everything, but I can do something.
The something I ought to do, I can do.
And by the grace of God, I will.

— Edward Everett Hale

I find that service to others gives me another dimension in my search for living a meaningful life. When I was in high school, I heard President John F. Kennedy say,

"Ask not what your country can do for you,
but what you can do for your country."

At age 14 there was not much I could do with this, but I never forgot it. In my senior year of high school I was instrumental in finding a senior project where about 50 students went to a private school for children with autism. Some of my classmates painted and repaired items, while others sat with the children and experienced autism firsthand. The following year, a college professor, Lynn Straub, said in a business class that we all have a responsibility as a citizen to give back to the world. These three incidents stand out in my mind even today as having been my impetus for wanting to serve others.

I, too, believe it is up to each of us to voluntarily give back to society. The first President Bush called volunteers "Points of Light." As a teacher it was a goal of mine to inspire students to enjoy giving to and doing for others. I became the advisor to an honorary group of senior students called "Ecivres" (service spelled backward). Our whole existence was based on finding service projects to give back to the school and community.

Later, in a different school, I advised the Key Club, the high school affiliate of Kiwanis International. The mission of this club is "to serve the community, create leaders and instill a 'love' for volunteerism." There were over 100 students in my club and they were doing one to three volunteer projects a month.

You don't have to have a college degree to serve.
You don't have to make
your subject and verb agree to serve.
You only need a heart full of grace.
A soul generated by love.

— Martin Luther King, Jr.

One of our largest projects, the Spirit of Christmas, was opened up to the entire student body. There were over 200 student volunteers from the high school, each in teams of three to eight students. Working with an outside social services agency, each team received a family to adopt for Christmas. The students provided gifts for each child in the family and a holiday dinner. Many times there was enough money to buy for the parents or for needed household items. Sometimes the students got donated items including Christmas trees and ornaments.

These teams contacted the families, raised the money, planned, shopped, and delivered the gifts and food. Unlike many other gift-giving opportunities, these high school students had a chance to meet the kids for whom they had purchased gifts and witness directly the joy they were bringing. It was one of those warm, fuzzy, emotional experiences which most of the students will hold with them for a lifetime. This event continued for almost 20 years with the number of teams and families adopted each year increasing. (In its final year we served 45 families.) The teams of students were often from middle- and upper-middle-class families, who had never been to the poor urban neighborhoods in and around San Diego. Reading their final reflection papers about their experiences was always my favorite part of the process. Many students admitted feeling guilty about all they had. Others said that it was just the beginning of a life of "giving back" to society. My heart melts….

Passing on my love for community service and helping others was one of the greatest rewards of my teaching career. Is it any wonder that the following quotes truly resonate with me?

We cannot build our own future
without helping others to build theirs.

— Bill Clinton

One of the deep secrets of life is that all
that is really worth the doing
is what we do for others.

— Lewis Carroll

An effort made for the happiness of others
lifts us above ourselves.

— Lydia M. Child

Great opportunities to help others seldom come,
but small ones surround us daily.

— Judith Kelman

BEING THANKFUL

*We can only be said to be alive in those moments
when our hearts are conscious of our treasures.*

— Thornton Wilder

"Happy Thanksgiving" is such a common greeting in November. Many of us have Thanksgiving Day traditions of going around the table sharing the things for which we are thankful. It doesn't have to end there — for me, being grateful is a daily goal. It keeps me optimistic and hopeful.

I had to spend over 12 months in bed. Those 365 + days of lying flat gave me much time for prayer, introspection, and long talks with God. I would like to share with you some of the things I have learned about being thankful. Some people refer to it as "an attitude of gratitude."

Breathe in — feel gratitude; breathe out — give thanks

— The Dalai Lama

This quote is at the top of my "To Do List" and under my "signature" on my e-mail — both are places where I know I will see this reminder several times daily. Some days I feel full-heartedly thankful, other days following this guidance with honesty is difficult. Nonetheless, I have found the words "thank you" to be immeasurably helpful while recuperating this year.

We tend to forget that happiness doesn't come
as a result of getting something we don't have,
but rather of recognizing and appreciating what we do have.

— Frederick Koenig

My surgery site may not have healed as quickly as I wanted and prayed for, but I found every day brighter when I named and was thankful for all the blessings around me.

I needed the quiet, no prison my bed,
but a beautiful valley of blessings instead....

Since I had the time, I started doing a little exploration on gratitude. Many people have researched and written about being grateful, thankful, and appreciative of their lives. One of those people is Oprah who has often talked about keeping gratitude journals since she was 15. She remembers a conversation with Maya Angelo when she was depressed about something (she could not remember what) that went something like this:

"Say Thank You **out loud**," encouraged Maya Angelo

"Thank you — but what am I saying thank you for?" asked Oprah.

"You're saying thank you," Maya said, "because your faith is so strong that you don't doubt that whatever the problem, you'll get through it. You're saying thank you because you know that, even in the eye of the storm, God has put a rainbow in the clouds. You're saying thank you because you know there's no problem created that can compare to the Creator of all things."

And to that I say, "Amen."

"Living in the space of thankfulness," as Oprah calls it, has turned my life around. There was a time when all I could see were the bad things happening to me. Negativity was everywhere — especially in my attitude. Then I started giving thanks for small things (a sunny day or a card from a friend), and the more thankful I became, the more significant my list became. I think that's because when I focused on the goodness in my life, God opened up windows and doors that allowed me to see more opportunities, relationships, and healing. I am learning to be more grateful no matter what happens in my life.

> *When one door closes another door opens;*
> *but we so often look so long and so regretfully*
> *upon the closed door,*
> *that we do not see the ones which open for us.*
> — *Alexander Graham Bell*

Mother Teresa talked about how grateful she was to the people she was helping, the sick and dying in the slums of Calcutta, because they enabled her to grow and deepen her spirituality. That's a different way of thinking about gratitude — gratitude for what we can give as opposed to what we receive.

Robert A. Emmons, Ph.D., is one of the leading scientific experts on gratitude. He is a professor of psychology at the University of California, Davis, and the founding editor-in-chief of The Journal of Positive Psychology. He is also the author of the book, *Thanks! How the New Science of Gratitude Can Make You Happier.*

Is gratitude really a science? I suppose it could be, but I do agree with much of what he has to say. Emmons recommends keeping a gratitude journal and listing just five things for which you are grateful every week. This practice works, I think, because it consciously and intentionally focuses our attention on developing more grateful thinking and helps guard against taking things for granted. Like Emmons, I believe that

> people who live a life of pervasive thankfulness really do experience life differently than people who cheat themselves out of life by not feeling grateful.

He further states that "the results (of keeping this journal) have been overwhelming." People who practice gratitude consistently report a host of benefits: **Physically,** they are less bothered by aches and pains, sleep longer and feel more refreshed upon waking; **Psychologically,** they are more alert and alive, have more optimism, happiness, and better self-esteem with less stress and anxiety; **Socially,** they are more helpful, generous, and compassionate; they are more forgiving, more outgoing, less lonely, and less isolated.

As Christians we know that with gratitude we benefit **spiritually** as well.

- **Gratitude allows us to draw closer to God**. We become a more active participant in our lives when we notice the positives, and this magnifies our relationship with God.

- **Gratitude allows us to celebrate the present** as we learn to be content in all things. (Philippians 4:11-13)

- **Gratitude and acknowledgment help us to recognize the miracles,** big and small, that happen in our lives each day.

- **Gratitude gives us a higher sense of self-worth**. It allows us to see how we've been supported and affirmed by God. When we are grateful, we have the sense that God is looking out for us. He has provided for our well-being, and we can begin to notice the network of people that God has placed in our lives — people who are responsible for helping us get to where we are today. We realize that other people see value in us and, therefore, we can change the way we see ourselves.

Circumstances don't determine character — they reveal it.

— Unknown

About their book, *Learning to Dance in the Rain*, BJ Gallagher and Mac Anderson say that "who we are as human beings is revealed most clearly during times of struggle, hardship, pain, and suffering. It's easy to be a good person when things are going great. But when times get tough, that's when you'll really find out the stuff you're made of."

Gratitude is not a fair-weather virtue.
True gratitude means appreciating your life
and thanking your God
… no matter what.

— Mac Anderson

OFF TO BATTLE...AGAIN

A strong woman believes that she
is strong enough to face her journey.
But a woman of strength has faith that
it is in the Journey
that she will become strong.

— Author Unknown
A Strong Woman Vs. A Woman of Strength

With every new crisis that I navigated successfully, I gained strength and confidence that I could make it through the next time. One of my biggest battles was in 1984 with the State of California. I was trying to qualify for one of the vehicles they had in a van pool ready for modification and available for people with disabilities. It took two years of appealing higher and higher through the red tape of the government, and the help of a sympathetic assemblyman, Randy Stirling, to qualify for a van from the State pool. It was hard not to feel rejected and sorry for myself every time I heard the answer "no" or "I'm sorry, you don't qualify." However, once I equipped myself with new and ambitious skills and a victor's heart, there was no stopping me! I was psychologically and physically ready to get a van I could drive myself, so I kept on fighting — appeal, after appeal, after appeal. I have learned to be a good fighter when it comes to my rights and the rights of others.

Being able to drive, I was in a better position to move ahead in some other important areas of my life. Having already won the fight to get my teaching job back (a very big struggle), I went back to school to earn my Master's degree and get an Administrative Credential. I was planning ahead and wanted to be ready for a career move if I needed one. This was my Plan B.... I had not thought I would also have to have a Plan C to face a completely different challenge....

Breast cancer affects one in four women, but we never think we will be the one. I certainly never did, but after finding a lump and getting a biopsy, I heard the words, "stage IV cancer."... Once the shock of the news subsided in me and my tears ran dry, I went on to have a mastectomy, endure chemotherapy, and receive radiation. During this time, I used imagery to attack those cancerous cells with the fury of a Samurai warrior. I envisioned an icon like in the old Pac-Man games, chomping bad cells. I ate well, read only positive material, and I learned meditation techniques. I chose not to join a support group, but rather to rally survivors and optimistic friends and family around me. My sister did all the research and shared with me only what I needed to know at the time in order to persevere and get through it victoriously. I am now a 22-year survivor.

Life with a disability is challenging at best. It seems that another barrier, roadblock, or obstacle is always just around the corner, and whether it is my health, my HMO, or the electric company, I know that I will always be strong enough to fight on. For me, the ever-present appeal process is just another step in my decision to always "choose life."

*Never allow a person to tell you no
who doesn't have the power to say yes.*

— Eleanor Roosevelt

Nothing is impossible; the word itself says, "I'm possible!"

— Audrey Hepburn

*Being defeated is often a temporary condition.
Giving up is what makes it permanent.*

— Marilyn Savant

The Early Years

Rehabilitation

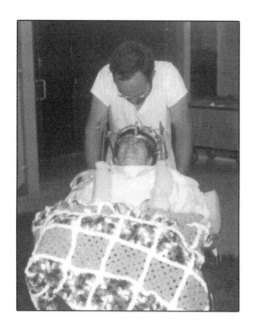

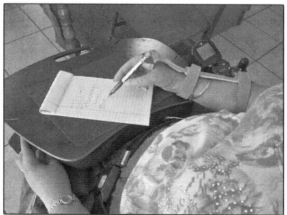

My Dogs

Heidi

Willie

Alex

Pacific

Ben

Teachers and Students

Sandy and Me

Pacific and Me
At School

Ben is Still Learning

My Vans
On the Road Again

My Family

"I get by with a little
help from my friends"

DISAPPOINTMENT

Give me strength, Lord, to finish well
and not allow life's disappointments,
(along with age, aches and pains),
to dampen my trust.
Amen

Despite my life's circumstances, I tend to believe in fairy tales and expect all my wishes to come true. For someone with high expectations like mine, disappointment is inevitable — and I have not been spared.

My first major disappointment, as noted, was the ending of my marriage. When I married, I had envisioned having a 50th wedding anniversary with Mike. I imagined children and grandchildren. I had been willing to give up my teaching career and leave my family and friends in San Diego to move to a smaller town in another state to begin a family. I had a dream, and I was going to do whatever it took to have it come true. My dream did not come true, and my divorce led to pain, sadness, and resentment.

Some people have the opportunity to begin again. I did have new opportunities and new people in my life that brought me wholeness, happiness, and new hope. That, however, did not take away from the loss and disappointment of losing "the family I never had."

———◦✿◦———

Then there is the obvious disappointment of missing out on an active life — the fresh air and natural beauty while camping, the earth underfoot when hiking, the feel of a racket in my hand when serving a tennis ball. I can no longer cut fabric and sew up a new skirt, learn a new piece of sheet music at the piano or enjoy making crafts for the holidays. I have found other ways to enjoy some of these things, but it does not take away the sadness of my being unable to experience these things firsthand.

———◦✿◦———

Because "quads" are unable to do weight-bearing exercise, osteoporosis is a common problem. I have broken many bones. People always look perplexed when I say I've broken my ankle or hip. It's not like I was skiing down a mountain over the weekend. Instead, it just takes raising my leg too high during range of motion activities for me to break a hip, or someone placing my foot against their leg and tugging on my pant leg to straighten them — at which point my ankle twists and breaks! I can't feel the pain of the broken bone, but I have learned to identify the problem by the spasms appearing in the rest of my body. Not only are my bones very brittle because of the osteoporosis, but they are also too fragile for surgery. My broken hips have never healed…

Because of my weak and brittle bones, disappointment also enveloped me when I realized that traveling had become too difficult and too risky for me. In each of three vacations, I ended up breaking multiple bones. The many transfers necessary in air travel, for example — transferring from my chair to the airport chair, then to the aisle chair, then to the seat — or, on the ground, just the mere transfer from wheelchair to bed without the ceiling lift I have at home — can lead to disaster. I get vicarious pleasure from seeing photographs and listening to stories of the trips my family and friends make, but it's not remotely the same as being able to absorb the sites, the sounds, the smells, and the ambience of the wider world.

The sudden disappointment of a hope leaves a scar
which the ultimate fulfillment of that hope
never entirely removes.

— Thomas Hardy

This is so true for me. Even as life moves ahead, often to a better place, the scar is still there.

We must accept finite disappointment,
but never lose infinite hope.

— Martin Luther King Jr.

Life's disappointments are harder to take
when you don't know any swear words.

— Calvin and Hobbes

WORDS TO LIVE BY

Plant Your Own Garden

There were many difficult and depressing times during the early years after my accident. During that time I was an emotional mess — confused, hurt, and lonely — and I had built a wall around my heart to protect me from further hurt. Then I read the following poem, and it changed my life.

COMES THE DAWN

by Jorge Luis Borges
(*originally in Spanish*)

After a while, you learn the subtle difference
between holding a hand and chaining a soul,
and you learn that love doesn't mean leaning
and company doesn't mean security.

And you begin to learn that kisses aren't contracts
and presents aren't promises.
and you begin to accept your defeats
with your head up and your eyes open
with the grace of a woman, not the grief of a child.

And you learn to build all your roads on today,
because tomorrow's ground is too uncertain for plans,
and futures have a way of falling down in mid-flight.

After a while you learn that even sunshine
burns if you get too much.
So you plant your own garden
and decorate your own soul
instead of waiting for someone to bring you flowers.

And you learn that you really can endure...
that you really are strong
and you really do have worth.

And you learn and learn...
with every goodbye you learn.

It pierced right through those thick barricades and spoke to me in a way that nothing else had. It captured pain and hopelessness, yet it turned it around and gave me hope, BIG HOPE — in the symbolic form of a flower garden. I knew that I, too, could take hold of my life and move forward with strength.

We often hear it said, "Bloom where you're planted." Well, my garden mantra became "Don't wait for someone to bring you flowers, plant your own garden!"

I took the advice of "planting my own garden," both figuratively and literally. After finding this poem, I repainted my house eliminating the masculine colors and bringing in light blues; I added flowered wallpaper and paintings of flowers, and I planted flowers in the garden. It was my way of "washing that man right out of my hair." In all the years since, I have continued to hang on to this mantra. I hang out in nurseries full of flowers all year round.

I found a local artist, Elizabeth Taft, whom I really like. She paints watercolors of Iris and I now have four of her paintings in my home. In fact, I have flowers in almost every room!

This feeling of empowerment has gone way beyond flowers. Now that I am reaching those "milestone" birthdays, I no longer need someone else to plan my parties; I can do it myself. When I am invited to events full of couples, I invite a friend or feel comfortable going alone. I no longer need others to help me feel whole. I have started looking for other people who are interested in attending plays, taking day trips, and rummaging through antique stores...

And when love came again, I was ready.

*A man sooner or later discovers that he is
the master-gardener of his soul,
the director of his life.*

— James Allen

*Did you know... that when you walk past a flower,
whether it be in somebody's garden or on a vacant hillside,
the flower will always smile at you.
The most polite way to respond, I've been told,
is to cheerfully return the smile.*

— Ron Atchison

AFFIRMATIONS & QUOTES
Positive Self-Talk

I use affirmations and quotes for motivation and inspiration. People do it all the time — post notes on their mirror ('remember to smile,' 'look people in the eyes') or on their refrigerator ('make healthy choices' or maybe a cartoon of someone on a scale). Others read daily meditations, quotes, or the Bible.

There are many styles of affirmations including mantras, incantations, or verbal rituals. Regardless of the name they're given, they are supposed to penetrate the subconscious mind and compel you to take action so that you achieve your goals.

Often when I read something that is inspirational, short, and positive, I copy it and paste it somewhere I can read it daily. I know that these quotes and phrases are not true to the definition of an affirmation, but they work for me.

As I mentioned earlier, my favorite daily affirmation is:

Breathe in—feel gratitude; breathe out—offer thanks.

— The Dalai Lama

This serves as a reminder until such time as I no longer need to be reminded. I also read this quotation by Vivian Greene every time I open my computer:

Life is not about waiting for the storm to pass...
It's about learning to dance in the rain.

This motivates me to learn "new dances."

———∞∞∞———

Affirmations are positive, specific statements that help me overcome self-sabotaging and negative thoughts. They're usually succinct, positive statements that target a specific area, behavior, or belief that I'm struggling with.

Many of us have negative thoughts, sometimes on a regular basis. When we have these thoughts, our confidence, mood, and outlook become negative, too. The problem with negative thoughts is that they can be self-fulfilling. Inside our heads, we talk ourselves into believing that we're not good enough. And, because of this, these thoughts drag down our personal lives, our relationships, and our careers.

This is why consciously doing the opposite, using positive affirmations, can be helpful. I try looking at positive affirmations this way — many of us do repetitive exercises to improve our body's physical health and condition. Affirmations are like exercises for our mind and outlook; these positive mental repetitions can reprogram our thinking patterns so that, over time, we begin to think, and act, in a new way.

I find that I can use affirmations in any situation where I'd like to see a positive change take place. Commonly, these might include times when I want to control negative feelings (such as frustration, anger, or impatience), improve my self-esteem, or increase my productivity.

Although I don't often use affirmations in this way, they are usually present tense with a personal pronoun being used, such as:

- I can do this!

- I am successful.

- I'm grateful for the job I have.

- I bring a positive attitude to work every day.

- I am excellent at what I do.

Repeating the affirmation several times a day is also part of the formula for success.

I found many different versions of the following quote on the Internet:

"Words of Wisdom…Points to Ponder…Inspirational Quotes…we all need them every now and then. These inspirational quotes sometimes leap out of the page from a newspaper, or a book or calendar, or emails, or even text messages in our cell phones. At certain times, they are just exactly what we need to hear; or they may just be the push that can change our lives by making us see a different perspective to things."

I encourage you to find a way to use affirmations or quotes in your own life. If you are anything like me, they will remind you of the person you want to become.

COMPANIONSHIP

The more one does and sees and feels,
the more one is able to do;
and the more genuine may be one's appreciation
of fundamental things
like home, and love, and understanding companionship.

— Amelia Earhart

I've always been a friendly person. I like being around people — one at a time, small groups or large groups. Maybe I "need" these friendships — I never really thought about it; I just enjoy being in relationship with all kinds of people.

I cultivated friendships with students at college, colleagues at school, with neighbors, with church members and others; but none of these is the same as finding the one special person with whom I wanted to spend the rest of my life. I was only 21 when I married Mike, and I was only 34 when he divorced me. In part, it was my other friendships that saved me.

I still felt very lonely. Eating dinner at the kitchen table alone, lying in bed watching a good program alone, enjoying a special dinner, or seeing some incredibly beautiful scenery alone was, and still is, hard beyond words. And then there were all the things I just never did anymore — spontaneous movies and other plans are difficult because so many of my friends are married. I had also been part of several couples groups including my Sunday school class, Tender Loving Couples. Now single, I dropped those groups, too, leaving me even more isolated and lonesome.

I had friends and family all around me, but there was still a big hole in my life.

Shortly after this time, when I was ridding my house of masculine colors, I met Sandy. She managed the paint store I was using and was a big help in choosing wall colors and wallpaper. She gave me a very reasonable quote for painting the inside of my house. I thought she felt sorry for me but she let me know later that it was because she wanted to get to know me better, and during the process we became friends.

Sandy was a single woman with no kids or other responsibilities. I was immediately drawn in by her outgoing personality and unstoppable energy. Everyone nicknamed her the "Energizer Rabbit." She had a skip to her step that was positive and fun. In addition, she was not afraid of my disability and was even interested in learning more.

When the painting in my home was done, we knew we would continue to see one another. The first time we got together we went to the zoo — I remember having fun and laughing uncontrollably. That was new for me and something missing from my life during the previous several years. As the years went on, Sandy introduced me to NFL football games (through season tickets to the Chargers), country music, and sushi. I introduced her to plays, card games, and high school sports. We both liked restaurants, concerts, and movies.

I finally found the companionship (other than my dogs) I craved. A problem unexpectedly arose, however. I knew that Sandy was gay and I began to feel uncomfortable — not with her sexuality, but with her intentions. I was in unfamiliar territory and I only wanted to be her friend, so we parted ways. I missed her, and I was sad and frustrated when thinking about her.

Then, a couple of years later, Sandy heard about my breast cancer surgery and came to visit at the hospital (neutral ground). We talked and laughed as if no time had passed. She continued to visit me at home more and more regularly, and we soon worked through my misgivings of having such a close gay friend. Several years later Sandy moved into my home. Four women, Sandy, my two live-in caregivers, and me) under the same roof can sometimes be challenging — but that's another story.

We had a loving and symbiotic relationship — one based on the mutual fulfillment of many needs. We knew one another's strong areas and we knew our weaknesses, and helping each other became very natural. Sandy loved to clean house and to garden (can you believe that?). While my caregiver got me through my two-hour morning routine, Sandy would have all the floors vacuumed, a load of laundry done, and the patios in front and back rinsed off and clean. I helped her with her bills and the budget for her store. She had a quick temper, and my quiet disposition could usually calm her down quickly. In addition to my personal care, Lupe and Nely (my caregivers of 28 and 15 years, respectively) did the majority of cooking, cleaning, and laundry. We were a well-oiled machine — everyone knew what to do.

I felt the joy come back into my life. I was able to make plans for vacations, order season tickets, and know ahead of time what

I would be doing the upcoming weekend. Although it was important to both Sandy and me to maintain relationships with our other friends and family, we were together most of the time. We took road trips and flew to Hawaii twice for vacation. She learned that nothing is ever easy when a disability is involved. In our first trip to Hawaii the sliding door fell off the accessible van we rented — and it was the only one available on the island. The next time we were there, my wheelchair motor broke, and Sandy pushed me around for several days before it could be repaired.

One day Sandy decided to trade in her SUV for a convertible. Then she convinced me to ride 500 miles up to San Francisco with the top down! (We pulled my wheelchair in a small trailer behind us.) I can still see my mom's face when we drove up to the house. Although fun, that car did not turn out to be as practical as she had hoped, so she then traded it in for a van that we converted with a lowered floor and lock-down spot for my wheelchair. My need for independence in getting around (driving my own van) was still important to me, but it was also nice to be able to be a passenger instead of always being the driver. We never sold the van, but Sandy's last car purchase was a used Porsche convertible. She liked the speed and the open air. Using a Hoyer lift, we would place me into the passenger seat and off we would go on regular Sunday afternoon drives in the sun.

It is hard to believe that fear almost kept me from the 15 years I shared with her.

There is not enough celebration of companionship.
Relationships aren't just about eroticism and sexuality.

— Francesca Annis

Then the bomb dropped. Sandy had been having a lot of pain in her upper abdomen for quite a while, and none of her trips to the doctor had brought her relief. Finally, after a night in the emergency room, two doctors returned to tell her that she was gravely ill with Stage IV colon cancer and that she was probably looking at two years of life *if* she had surgery and chemotherapy. We were in shock! It was recommended that she leave her job and focus on what she wanted to do in the time she had left. She wasn't even 50 years old.

Sandy's first year after surgery was not too difficult. She still had strength, vitality, her sense of humor, and her love of life. Once she had been on chemo for several full courses, however, her energy dwindled, as did her ability to concentrate for long periods of time. Reading, which she loved, was especially difficult because it was hard for her to focus. It was referred to as "chemo brain."

It's hard to explain what it's like to help a loved one live out numbered days. Although she acted like a trooper, she always said she felt like a time bomb ready to go off. It was a gift to me that I could be with her through this lonely and often painful process. I tried to distract her, choose activities and foods she could still enjoy, and just be with her.

The Mechanics of Dying…. Choosing to lovingly care for her was like steering a plane into a mountain as gently as possible. The crash is imminent, it's how you spend your time on the way down that counts.

—from *Hotel on the Corner of Sweet and Misery*

Because there was so little I could actually do to help her, my sister moved in with us for the last two weeks. Hospice also sent a wonderful team to assist us through these long days and nights. As it takes a village to raise a child, it also takes a village to help someone die comfortably and with dignity.

Sandy had made peace with her prognosis and was ready to go home to God. Over 400 people attended the "Celebration of Life" we held at our church. It had a Hawaiian theme — everyone in attendance was asked to wear shorts, flip-flops, and a Hawaiian shirt in her honor. It was a joyous occasion with lots of wonderful storytelling and reminiscing, just as Sandy had wanted.

God blessed me by bringing Sandy into my life. It was only for a few years, but they were rich, life-giving years.

*Some people come into our lives
and leave footprints on our hearts
and we are never ever the same.*

— Flavia Weedn

WORK WITH WHAT YOU'VE GOT

The following story is taken from the book, *Barefoot Runner*, by Paul Rambali.

Ken Mierke is an exercise physiologist and world champion tri-athlete. He also has muscular dystrophy. Ken learned from his dad to love sports, but he was overweight, disabled and slow when he moved. In order to make up for his weak leg, he learned to examine everything about a sport and find a better way, even with a disability, for him to do it. In basketball he practiced three pointers and a deadly hook shot. In tennis he couldn't sprint across the court so he developed a ferocious serve and return. "If I couldn't outrun you, I'd outthink you," he says," I'd find your weakness and make it my strength." When he began to compete in triathlons, he studied videos of Kenyan barefoot runners and developed techniques that allowed him to become a world champion. Later as a coach, he produced eleven national champion tri-athletes.

I love this story. He is not being defined by his disability, nor is it confining him to a "lesser life." He has learned to work with what he's got.

First, I had to learn just what *I* had to work with. I tried to do that by getting to know myself — my strengths and my weaknesses — and by learning about what my body could and could not do. I am continually taking stock and re-acquainting myself with changes that occur over time. It is all part of self-knowledge.

Starting in rehabilitation, I learned *how* my body worked and *what* it could accomplish; I also learned medical terminology and a whole new way of looking out for myself physically. For instance, my temperature regulator isn't very effective, and it's easy for me to overheat. If I don't cool down, I can go into dysreflexia, which can cause a sudden onset of excessively high blood pressure and a headache; or maybe, just my face turns red, and my nose runs. The same thing can happen if I'm too close to a fireplace or campfire. I need someone to check my skin because I cannot feel the heat and can burn easily. Once I was seated near a fireplace that heated the metal side piece of my wheelchair, which in turn burned my thigh. I had not felt any heat nor pain. It was only when I got undressed that I found the nasty results.

I pay attention to what my body is telling me on a daily basis. I have to. Even a twitching finger or a stuffy nose can be telling me that my ankle is turned or my catheter is blocked. I had to learn new warning signs for pain and discomfort. Armed with this knowledge, I can be proactive in my care, better able to speak with doctors and do research.

It has also been important for me to learn my coping mechanisms — how I cope in difficult situations. I know that I tend to get very busy — it's an easy way to be in denial and not face a painful emotion or an uncomfortable set of circumstances. This is especially true when I rush through the grieving process because the sadness often hurts too much. I also recognize that writing this book and listening to 50 books this past year while in bed were both avoidance mechanisms for my unhappiness, disappointment, and boredom in being confined to lying flat on my back.

On the other hand, I am fortunate to have been born with a positive outlook. It is part of who I am and my accident did not take it away. I know it is one of God's gifts for me. I live in His grace, the glass is always half-full, and I can usually see the "up side" of any situation.

I gravitate toward sayings such as:

"Every cloud has a silver lining"

"Bloom where you are planted"

"When God gives you lemons, ask for tequila and salt"

"There is always a light at the end of the tunnel"

"This, too, shall pass"

And I believe them! This does not mean that I don't get angry or depressed. For the most part, it just means that I have confidence that, with God's help, I can get through whatever comes my way.

We all need to learn to "work with what we've got," to emphasize our strong suits and minimize our weaknesses. My strengths include being sociable, communicating well, having strong leadership and organizational skills and a love of mentoring students. I needed to claim and use these skills when I originally returned to work, when I looked for places to volunteer –and now, in retirement.

I always prayed for a better singing voice, but that was not to be. I will never be a marathoner, but I can support those who run.

*People often say that this or that person
has not yet found himself.
But the self is not something one finds,
it is something one creates.*

— Thomas Szasz

INDEPENDENCE

Promise me you'll always remember:
You're braver than you believe,
and stronger than you seem, and smarter than you think.

— Christopher Robin to Pooh

There are many ways to help people feel independent, and in time, I learned which of those ways were best for me. I know of many people, paraplegics and quadriplegics alike, who choose to live on their own and have caregivers come in both mornings and evenings. That gives them the independence they want.

For me, however, it was important that I could get up at 4:30 a.m. every week day because it took me two hours to shower, dress, do hair and makeup, and swallow a protein drink before getting on my way to school. I also wanted the flexibility of going to bed at different times depending on what plans I had — taking an evening class, going to dinner and a movie, or just getting down early to give my body a rest.

In order to accommodate a flexible schedule, I chose to hire live-in caregivers. In this way I was sure that they would be here early enough in the morning, could accomplish things during the day like housecleaning, laundry, food shopping and meal preparation, and still have some free time before I got home from school in the afternoons.

Again, independence means something different for everyone, but for someone with the limitations I have this arrangement works best for me. There is a fine line between independence and the need for people.

I have probably mentioned it far too often, but being paralyzed in all four limbs generally means that there is not much I can do *by* or *for* myself. It is one thing to have to ask somebody to do the big things for me like getting me up for the day, but it is downright tiring for both me and others if I have to call for assistance every time I'm thirsty or I want a different station on the TV. Fortunately, over the past 30 years technology has played a big part in giving me, and others like me, more independence. I use voice activation for my computer and my remote control; I have a special telephone and a front door that can be opened with the push of a button. One of my friends, also quadriplegic and a former engineer, had his whole house pretty much controlled by voice — his bedroom curtains, the coffee pot, and all the lights and electronics in his home. With a severe disability, it is a wonderful feeling to accomplish even the simple things independently. I hate the feeling of being a burden on others, even if they are being paid.

Although I enjoyed every bit of independence I could squeeze out of my life in the first several years after my accident, there was one area I was still determined to conquer. I was craving more than just controlling the environment inside my home — I wanted to drive! I hired people to drive me to school, meetings and social events for six years after my accident. After those long six years, my right arm, the only thing I could move besides my head, finally got strong enough to take driving lessons!

Charlie Scott, a pilot during his younger years and an engineer by profession, founded the company, Driving Systems Incorporated, and designed the "Scott Van" in the late 1970s. Using a Ford Econo-line Van, Charlie had ingeniously created a joystick method of driving similar to the airplanes he used to fly. With this design, a wheelchair moves into the driver's position and locks down. The joystick has a post from the floor of the van up to the driver's elbow with a small platform to support the forearm. The hand fits into another device, and together with the joystick post, allows the disabled driver to steer the van, accelerate and brake. Depending on the driver's disability, there were several possibilities for how other driving functions could be accomplished. (www.drivingsystems.com)

I use a headpiece attached to the ceiling with six little posts which can turn on blinkers, switch gears, set the cruise control, or honk the horn. In addition, I have a panel of buttons that I can push with a mouse stick. This allows me to start the ignition, open windows, turn on the radio, and much more. The van's seven mirrors help me to see all the areas around the van that are difficult for me to see because my neck is fused. There are other vans and newer designs now, but this one still works best for me.

It took me over 1000 miles of practice and two very patient driving instructors to be ready to attempt the driving test. As I pulled out of the driveway with the testing instructor I cut off a car coming into a blind spot I didn't know I had. I failed before even reaching the street. I added another mirror, practiced another week, and finally passed my next driving test — thanks be to God!

Now *this* was independence! "On the Road Again" by Willie Nelson became my new favorite song!

DOG = BEST FRIEND

Until one has loved an animal,
a part of one's soul remains unawakened.

— Anatole France

My search for independence did not end with my driver's license. It also catapulted me into the world of dogs. I was now looking for new ways to accomplish seemingly simple tasks like turning on lights, moving things out of my way, and picking up dropped items. It may seem like my goals were moving from the sublime to the mundane — but, oh my, how far from the truth that is. To a person with no disabilities, these simple tasks may seem commonplace since they are easy to do, but to a person with my handicaps, they can become monumental. Assistance dogs became the solution to my search for yet more independence.

I waited a long time to be accepted to the Canine Companions for Independence (CCI) program for assistance dogs. But unfortunately after I started my two-week "boot camp," I became ill and had to drop out. I was disappointed beyond belief. Friends suggested that I adopt a dog from a shelter and have it trained. I tried this with two wonderful dogs, but ended up passing them along to other good families because they weren't going to work out for my needs.

That's when I met Alex, a large golden retriever, being released from CCI because his first owner had died. My heart melted at first sight — he was beautiful, gentle, affectionate and really well trained. Alex went to my high school with me daily and seemed to know just which of my students needed his attention. He did everything I needed, and more. I had had dogs growing up and loved them, but I had never loved one as much as I came to love Alex. He went everywhere with me — we were definitely partners.

An incident that illustrates this partnership occurred one weekend while we were attending a conference at a retreat center in the mountains. Everyone was taking the stairs from the dining hall down to the meeting room; I had to take the service road some distance away. On the way my wheelchair went over wet leaves, which sent me into a spinning roll down the hill backward. This was my first and only time to fall out of my wheelchair. I let out a scream and Alex, who had taken a shortcut with someone else, heard me. He came running across a big expanse of lawn bringing everyone else with him. I had my own "knight in shining armor" coming to my rescue!

Pacific was my second service dog, this time from Tender Loving Canines Assistance Dogs (TLCAD). He was a very intelligent, athletic yellow lab. He never met a ball he didn't like! I remember being in a shopping center parking lot late at night and dropping the keys that open the back doors of my van. Before I had a minute to think, Pacific went under the van, got the keys and put them on my lap. He, too, was always getting me out of jams — and allowing me my independence.

Service Dogs usually know 80 to 100 verbal commands. Most importantly, they are intuitive and seem to know when they're needed and what needs to be done. My dogs have been magical creatures that made a large difference in my life. That is why I decided I wanted to be part of the nonprofit organization, TLCAD, which blessed me with this amazing gift. It is so obvious that God is in the middle of every placement — the perfect dog, with its perfect partner!

I am now partnered with my third service dog, Ben. He is a yellow English Labrador Retriever. All of my dogs have had very different personalities, and so far he is the most playful and the most affectionate. At the same time, his skills are amazing. One day while shopping, he even managed to put my ATM card into the slot in the ATM machine all by himself! Go Ben!

HE IS JUST MY DOG

He is my other eyes that can see above the clouds; my other ears that hear above the winds. He is the part of me that can reach out into the sea.

He has told me a thousand times over that I am his reason for being; by the way he rests against my leg; by the way he thumps his tail at my smallest smile; by the way he shows his hurt when I leave without taking him.

When I am wrong, he is delighted to forgive. When I am angry, he clowns to make me smile. When I am happy, he is joy unbounded. When I am a fool, he ignores it. When I succeed, he brags. Without him, I am only another man. With him, I am all-powerful.

He is loyalty itself. He has taught me the meaning of devotion. With him, I know a secret comfort and a private peace. He has brought me understanding where before I was ignorant. His head on my knee can heal my human hurts.

His presence by my side is protection against my fears of dark and unknown things. He has promised to wait for me...whenever... wherever...in case I need him. And I expect I will — as I always have.

He is just my dog.

— **Gene Hill**

PATIENCE

Patience is the ability to count down before you blast off.

— Carol Buchner

I used to be incredibly impatient. I was a Type-A Personality, always busy, usually multitasking and very picky about things. I was mostly impatient with slow-moving, slow-talking, lazy people.

Then all of a sudden I couldn't even scratch my nose by myself! Now that I'm in a wheelchair, I find myself sitting without accomplishing something far more than I ever knew possible. I am often just waiting. I hate that! It is very frustrating for me to wait on someone to put a CD in the player so I can listen to a book or to open the back door so I can go out on the patio.

Because I have to ask someone to do or get things for me all the time, I find it easy to lose patience with myself *and* other people. It can be a huge problem and can lead to much discord and disappointment. I still pray for patience regularly.

Definition — Patience is the ability to tolerate waiting, delay, or frustration without becoming agitated or upset. It is the ability to control your emotions or impulses and proceed calmly when faced with difficulties. It comes from the Latin word *pati* which means to suffer, to endure, to bear. (How appropriate is that!)

Developing patience requires persistence and effort; needless to say, it does not come easily to me.

How can a society that exists on instant mashed potatoes, packaged cake mixes, frozen dinners, and instant cameras teach patience to its young?

— Paul Sweeney

It is probably harder these days to be patient than it has ever been. In today's world of technological advancements, we can obtain, experience, and consume practically anything we want almost immediately.

Yet I believe if I want to reach my goals, have successful relationships, and achieve personal peace, patience is worth working for. I have learned that if something is worthwhile it probably cannot take place right away. It takes time, dedication, and effort to achieve; so perhaps in this day and age more than ever, patience **is** a virtue.

There are three situations where I know that learning patience has been a must in my life. One occurs when I have had to spend long periods of time waiting for wounds to heal, or for illnesses to subside. Another is in watching expectantly for the extra pounds to start melting away when I'm attempting to lose weight. The third is while I'm working through the grieving process — which **cannot** be rushed. This is true not only of the grief that accompanies losing a friend or loved one, but in **any** situation involving a deep loss, whether of a marriage one had counted on — or of one's taken-for-granted ability to walk or feed oneself.

But perhaps the most important area for me has been to be patient with caregivers and other health-care professionals. My daily routine and my very life depend on how I treat others — and patience is always required!

After all these years of teaching teenagers and being confined to a wheelchair, I have had many more opportunities to develop patience than most people. Sometimes it's hard to find the benefits of being paralyzed, but learning patience has been one of them! (Getting to the front of the line at a concert or an amusement park is another....)

It is said that patience, in and of itself:

- Helps reduce stress and makes us happier, healthier people. When I practice patience, I don't get as angry, stressed, or overwhelmed. I am more in control of my emotions and in a better position to deal with difficult situations.

- Helps us make better decisions. When I am practicing patience, I take the time to assess the situation, see the big picture, and weigh the pros and cons. The chances of making a big mistake lessen because I try to avoid making a decision in haste.

- Helps us become more understanding and compassionate. Patient people take the time to process what they go through and are better able to determine what it takes to overcome obstacles.

Wheelchair Wisdom: Here are a few tips that I learned and re-learned to become a more patient person. Although the examples are mine, many of the bullet items I found at **www.essential lifeskills.ne**t. There is a host of good information on the Internet, but these ideas best fit my own experience.

- **Take a day, and make patience my goal for the entire day**. I make an effort to take my time and think about everything I asked others to do for me. I try to put myself in their shoes. And when I do that, I really see what a pest I can be!

- **Plan ahead**. When I have the tendency to rush around and try to hurry things up, want things done immediately, or can't wait for things to take their natural course, I *STOP*. I take several deep breaths before I act or react, and I plan ahead for these situations. For example, if I am in a long lineup at the grocery store or in heavy traffic, I plan ahead so I will not get worked up. I keep a book, e-reader, or an iPod ready to go.

- **Practice delayed gratification**. When I want to ask for that dessert, new clothes, or another electronic toy, I try to stop and think about it first. Maybe I don't need or want any of them that badly after all. I can save myself some money and unnecessary calories, or I can wait for something more important that I need or want.

- **Think before I speak**. I have had my feelings hurt many times when people blurt out the first thought that comes into their heads. It is often hurtful. When I am patient, however, I can pause and go over what I want to say and avoid hurting or offending others.

Patience has definitely been a valuable and necessary character trait for me to cultivate. It is a trait that may appear to be passive, but it is actually a very powerful form of active self-discipline.

Learn the art of patience.
Apply discipline to your thoughts when they become anxious
over the outcome of a goal.
Impatience breeds anxiety, fear, discouragement, and failure.
Patience creates confidence, decisiveness,
and a rational outlook,
which eventually leads to success.

— Brian Adams

A handful of patience is worth more than a bushel of brains.

— Dutch Proverb

One moment of patience may ward off great disaster.

— Chinese Proverb

TEACHING AND LEARNING

We cannot always build the future for our youth,
but we can build our youth for the future.

— Franklin Delano Roosevelt

Everyone is a teacher at some time or in some capacity — I chose to make a career of it. And, of course, I wanted to be good at it. I strived to be knowledgeable and motivational in my subject area. Beyond that, I wanted to inspire, encourage, and empower students to reach their fullest potential — not just in my class — but in their all-around lives. I tried daily to honor and affirm who they were.

"They may forget what you said,
but they never forget how you made them feel."

I've always tried to remember that. In a career span of almost 40 years, there are too many memories to record here, but perhaps I can group some of them by lessons I gleaned from them. It is interesting for me to note that the following examples are from both before and after my accident. Disability or not, teaching and learning always went together.

In my first year of teaching I was assigned to a special education class of 12 students with behavioral problems. (There were not the same individual or classroom designations for "Special

Education" then as there are now.) I was not trained as a special education teacher, but because of my Psychology major I was considered "equipped enough to handle" these out-of-control seventh and eighth graders. I started in January as their third teacher that year. I was **not** prepared! I worked with the school psychologist on Behavior Modification and learned how to put it into practice. With that and other new strategies, I learned more in that one semester about teaching students (which is different from teaching subject matter) than in all my student teaching experiences. They offered me a contract for the following year — I declined.

—◆◆◆—

In the mid-1970s the "Boat People" started to arrive in San Diego. There were two million refugees, mostly from South Vietnam, who had escaped imprisonment or worse when the U.S. withdrew all troops. The Vietnamese who were our allies knew that they would have no life under communist rule. They were referred to as "Boat People" because they literally left everything behind and escaped by boat to nearby freighters and to other coastal countries. They eventually made their way to countries around the world.

Many of these families settled in the community around the high school where I taught. Up to this point, my only knowledge of the Vietnamese War was the accounts I was seeing on the nightly news. Now I was hearing their stories up close and personal — and they were tragic. The first waves of students were, for the most part, the children of government officials and wealthy families. They spoke English and were polite, hard-working, and extremely appreciative of their teachers and their opportunities for education. They were also the first group of students to invite me into their homes for celebrations and special occasions. These families helped me learn how integral the family unit can be in the success of their students. They also helped me feel comfortable as "the teacher" outside the classroom.

From this point until my retirement, I often became a "second mom" for kids from other cultures. Their moms may or may not speak English, but it is not the language that is the stumbling block for many parents as much as the culture shock. First-generation children growing up in the United States are far more ready to jump into American customs than are their parents, as has been true throughout history of the offspring of an immigrant generation. This oftentimes results in misunderstandings and family clashes. I became the *go to* person for many of my students — mostly girls. I was mainly a listener, but a learner, too. I kept the letter below because it affirmed the relationships I felt with many students.

From a male Chinese student ready to graduate:

Dear Ms. Timmins,

As my senior year comes to an end, it is sad to think about the people I will leave behind. It is most difficult to think about leaving you; your presence in my high school experience has been a great gift. Throughout life people encounter many special people, but there is always one extra special person that makes a more significant impact on life. That extra special person I consider you, Ms. Timmins.

Thank you for being such a caring mother-like figure in the midst of school horrors. You have always been so attentive to me and what is happening in my life. Your closeness throughout the past few years has become a true blessing. I am always so happy to be able to help you; working with you has not only been a learning experience, but also a significant impact on how I view teachers.

Thank you for being a contributor to my positivism and inspiration to work hard...

Sincerely yours, Stephen

———⟨∾⟩———

Although I was a teacher, it became evident to me over and over that I was also a learner — and not only from my students. A totally unexpected area of learning came with my service dogs, Alex and Pacific. The resting place in my classroom that Alex chose was a foamy bed under a table behind my desk. Pacific, on the other hand, chose the spot under my desk where his nose and eyes could peer into the classroom full of students. Although they appeared to be sleeping most of the time, they both kept their ears and nose on full alert at all times and knew what was going on.

On occasion I would have Pacific deliver No. 2 pencils for testing to students who didn't have one. (That only lasted until too many students said they forgot their pencils because they wanted a special one from Pacific!) As trained, my service dogs would leave the area behind my desk only if called — except one day when Pacific was aware of a "situation" I was having with a very irritated student. It seems that nothing would quiet her down, so he took it upon himself to come around from behind his area — crossed right in front of me — and lay down at her feet. I was shocked! He was being "disobedient" and, worse yet, he was rewarding the student for her poor behavior by being near her. My first instinct was to correct him, but I'm glad I caught myself. This student was now quiet, calm, AND WORKING! This time, and others to follow, I decided to learn from my dog that I could trust in his knowing instinct....

Although this particular incident has stayed with me over the years, I began to see the calming effect my dogs had on so many people in general. Teachers came in during their prep periods for a "fur fix," as it was lovingly called, and students were allowed to come in before school, during lunch, and after school to play with them. I quickly recognized that it was often those students who most needed their unconditional love.

—*φφφ*—

I learned another big lesson about classroom management from Father Bill Mahedy, a priest friend of mine, while taking his class, "How to Be a Christian at Work." One of the "pearls" I took away from that class was the suggestion to invite Jesus into my classroom with me each day. I did that every morning when I crossed the threshold. Don't get me wrong, this did not keep students from misbehaving, but it did keep me from responding poorly! A side benefit to that daily routine: although other teachers became nervous when an administrator was going to observe and evaluate, it never bothered me — I was used to having a far more important observer with me already!

—*φφφ*—

During many of my years teaching, I was the advisor to the Student Government (ASB) class and the Cheerleading squads. These students were active, vibrant, and smart. It took a lot to keep up with them, but a different student/teacher relationship and bond was created — largely because we worked together on tasks like sports rallies, dances, changing school policies, and student elections. We covered topics such as management skills and leadership training, and I tried to give them the trust and independence they needed to be leaders. This is very different from teaching typical classes because the dynamics change; they knew I trusted them with planning and carrying out "real life" events.

Another service group I advised was the Ecivres. At the end of each year, I would have them write themselves a letter with ideas of where they wanted to be in 10 years. I kept their letters and 9½ years later sent them back. Many contacted me at that time, and some still have those letters today. I learned to look for this type of relationship with students in all my classes, not just the elite few. Breaking the traditional teacher/student role can be transformative on both sides.

From an Ecivers in her RSVP to my retirement party

Mrs. Timmins,

… I remember you treating us like we were your friends (not just students), which was a real honor for a teenager. I try to emulate that in my role as a school nurse.

I kept a newspaper article titled "She Is Out To Prove She Can Still Teach" from the San Diego Union, 1979. It is stapled to the wall near my desk and I often look at it when I need encouragement through a hard time (If you could still teach, so could I!). You definitely impacted my life, and I still think about you often.

Barb, Class of 1975

I have been invited to reunions, family dinners, college graduations, wedding showers, weddings, baby showers, and kids' first birthday parties. I always tried to attend. Nowadays I get "friend"ed on Facebook!

From another student at graduation:

Dear Ms. Timmins,

… As I prepare to graduate, I can't help but remember how important your help, support, encouragement, love and care for me has been in getting through high school successfully. Your mentorship throughout my time at Serra helped guide me through challenges and inspired me to do great things. More importantly, your simple but amazing example of perseverance and courage in the midst of trial has been a source of motivation for me to conquer obstacles that I encounter, no matter how great they are... May God bless you richly for it!

Sincerely, Terence

And again, my heart melts…. Is this why we teach?

———

As my career ended last year, it is the friendships with my past students that I called upon to help me celebrate my retirement. Instead of the traditional ways to retire — have a party with your colleagues, or slip out quietly with no hype — I chose to *end* my career with the very students with whom I *shared* my career. I contacted a couple dozen students with whom I was still in touch, and with their help and that of the booming social media, soon had a core group of past students, student aides, and student teachers from two different schools with whom to rejoice. They ranged in age from 18 to 55! Most still live nearby, but one cheerleader flew in from Illinois. Even some of their moms, with whom I worked along the way, came along. **It was everything I hoped it would be — and more.**

Their stories took me back through the years as if I were on the bullet train. My emotions ran the gamut from laughter to tears, and I felt like a proud mom hearing of all their accomplishments and successes. It is hard to believe that some of them are ready to retire! What? How can that be possible?

For all I've learned from my students over the years, it is nice to hear that I left them with new attitudes, skills, and knowledge. And how lucky I am to be hearing from them now instead of having these comments said as an epitaph or in a eulogy! Here is one more of the stories they have shared with me throughout the years, and at retirement:

From college-age Teacher's Assistant

Dear Chris—

I met you at a time of profound transition in my life… I remember being in the classroom with you, experiencing how you held a respectful space for students and staff, how you set the bar high, celebrated the successes of those who met it, and supported everyone to do their absolute best. I remember much of my life falling apart while working during that time, but being able to shine brightly working with you. ..

I remember laughing out loud, heads down, bellies shaking. I remember finishing each other's thoughts and many knowing glances. I remember tolerance and forgiveness when I couldn't always show up with my best. That touches my heart the most and has been the most life-changing for me. Your generosity may have saved my life.

With much love, Lisa

One hundred years from now, it will not matter
what kind of car I drove,
what kind of house I lived in,
or how much money I had in the bank...
But that the world may be a better place
because I made a difference in the life of a child.

— Forest Witcraft

LET YOUR LIGHT SHINE

I think a hero is an ordinary individual who finds strength to persevere and endure in spite of overwhelming obstacles.

— Christopher Reeve

As a teacher, to be considered an inspiration is truly an honor and a compliment. These kind words are also spoken by others over a handshake, a cup of coffee, or in cards and letters. At these times I often feel embarrassed. After all, I don't feel special. I just keep on going, one day at a time.

Perhaps Christopher Reeve had the answer. "Overcomers" are not necessarily special. They are often ordinary people who have been placed in extraordinary circumstances and have been given strength to succeed in difficult times or situations. I concede that I have, by the Grace of God, learned to meet my challenges with a positive outlook, but it can be uncomfortable to be placed "on a pedestal" or held in such esteem. It seems that there is an assumption that I have accomplished something that others would never be able to do. On the contrary, other people *can* do it, too. They just don't know it because they have never been put to the test.

Having such an obvious disability is a blessing and a curse. Sometimes, my challenges help others open up about their problems, and we can help one another. At other times, people will tell me about some problem they are experiencing and then say, "Oh, but it is nothing compared to what you have to deal with." That is not at all true, and it is at this point that I feel I need to give a meaningful response. I am certain everyone suffers pain in some form or another, and some may have "silent or hidden" health issues or problems. No one should compare the magnitude or degree of one type of pain over another. Who is to say, for example, that a broken neck out-trumps drug addiction? Both are paralyzing. As Nick Vujic so astutely points out in his book, *Life Without Limits:*

"Pain is not a competition."

I do believe that we need mentors, heroes, and people who are inspirational to us. They encourage us to strive for lofty goals — to be better people. I appreciate the people in my life who inspire me, so I hope I've been able to do that for others. I am grateful that my life's journey has taken me from a time and place when I was overwhelmed and felt sorry for myself (even suicidal), to a place where I try to be a source of inspiration. I feel that I am fulfilling one of God's purposes for my life — and that's a good thing!

1994 INAUGURAL SPEECH

Nelson Mandela

Our deepest fear is NOT that we are inadequate.
Our deepest fear is that we are powerful beyond measure.
It is our light, not our darkness that frightens us.
We ask, who am I to be brilliant,
gorgeous, talented and fabulous?

Actually, who are you NOT to be?
You are a child of God.
Your playing small doesn't serve the world.
There's nothing enlightened about shrinking
so that other people won't feel insecure around you.

We were born to make manifest
the glory of God that is within us.
It's not just in some of us, it's in everyone.
And as we let our own light shine,
we unconsciously give other people permission
to do the same.

As we are liberated from our own fear,
our presence automatically liberates others.

I have kept a copy of this part of Mandela's speech in my files for all these years because it says something crucial to me. It speaks to me of how so many people, me included, feel about "letting our lights shine." I lean toward being shy about my accomplishments, and I am definitely not comfortable bragging about anything I've done or achieved. I guess that's why compliments are sometimes difficult for me. In the process of writing this book, I have re-learned that:

We were born to make manifest the glory of God
that is within us.
It's not just in some of us, it's in everyone.
And as we let our own light shine,
we unconsciously give other people permission
to do the same.

———

The nurse at my school has a poster with the following words hanging in her office. I know she meant them for the young eyes and minds of our students, but I took them to heart as well. I wanted to emulate the essence of these words — or at least model them — in my own life.

Watch your thoughts, they become words.
Watch your words, they become your actions.
Watch your actions, they become habits.
Watch your habits, they become character.
Watch your character, it becomes your destiny.

— Frank Outlaw

PEOPLE WHO NEED PEOPLE

People,
people who need people
are the luckiest people in the world.
We're children, needing other children
and yet letting a grown-up pride
hide all the need inside —
acting more like children than children.

— "People" from the musical and movie
Funny Girl, Lyrics by Jule Styne

I grew up with the German ethic of self-sufficiency: "If you want to get it done, do it yourself!" I didn't think that *needing* people was a very positive trait. In fact, when the movie *Funny Girl* came out, I didn't like this song. I didn't understand it. Now I realize my good fortune in being someone who needs people.

When you need people, it brings others into your life. Because I need people's help to do so many things, I get to meet people I would never have met otherwise. I get to hear their stories. There are times when I need someone to open a door at a shopping mall. Typically I wouldn't talk to huge guys with tattoos and chains, but in this situation I ask for their assistance, and they respond — very happily and courteously. It is a treat when my helpers turn out to be fun, polite, and compassionate. Another stereotype broken down....

My caregivers are another example of the benefit of meeting people that I may otherwise never have met. By the nature of their work, they quickly become intimately involved in my life, and I end up learning so much about them and from them. I learned Spanish so I could hire Hispanic women, because I believed them to be naturally compassionate, extremely good caregivers, and easy to find here in San Diego. It was a win-win situation. Another good example is Miki. She was one of my caregivers who, being very different from me, would not have been someone I would have chosen as a friend. Yet she turned out to be wonderful. She blessed and cleansed my house with white sage; she was a Russian language major and a self-professed Lesbian white witch. I was the one who was blessed to have known her.

The list goes on. With the help and encouragement of school friends, I challenged my school district to be able to return to work as a quadriplegic woman in a wheelchair. The district doctors told me that I should retire because my health was in jeopardy as a weak immune system would make me vulnerable to any life-threatening illnesses I might pick up from my students. The HR department had never heard of anyone else with my degree of disability teaching in a public school. Luckily, I had read the book and seen the movie, *The Other Side of the Mountain*, and knew of Jill Kinmont. She was an Olympic skier from California, who broke her neck and still pursued and attained a college degree, a teaching credential, and a job. She made the way for me (and others) so that we could follow her path as a teacher with a disability. I would like to think that in my life I have also done something that would set the stage for helping others pursue their own dreams.

Because I am now so keenly aware that I need people, I am more open to friends and strangers than I have ever been before. I better understand that needing people and serving people are two symbiotic sides of the same relationship. When I put myself *out there* and let others know that I need help, I am providing an opportunity for someone else to assist me, thereby giving them access to serving another. Many people, including me, thrive on being able to help others. When we ask for help, we allow others that chance to show compassion and have a purpose.

I also believe everyone needs people from whom they can draw inspiration, motivation, and encouragement. These individuals can be real — someone we know or have read about — or fictitious people or characters we've only heard about. Be ready — the exact individual might be closer than you think! I also think we can all be an encouragement to someone else by being willing to share ourselves and our stories more freely.

Mentors, heroes, and idols are important in our lives, just as Joni Eareckson Tada, a woman my age who is also quadriplegic, has been in mine. I admire her tremendously for all that she has been able to make happen both in her own life and in the disabled community globally. Now that I have finished one book, I can hardly fathom that she has written 70!

Being someone who needs people also opened me up to other women I knew, or knew of, who became my mentors. I have learned some of my biggest lessons from them. This list includes my Listeners and Encouragers for this book: *Dr. Donna Brooks, Jan Daugherty, BJ Gallagher, Gloria Lewis, Shirley Moore, Janet Allen Shaw*, and *Mary Thompson*. My list also includes the Mentors on my Journey: *Cathy Conheim, Joni Eareckson Tada, Jill Kinmont, Dr. Kris Laverty*, and *Rev. Patricia Moore*. More information on these women can be found in my Acknowledgments.

I also admire Christopher Reeve. He is a hero and inspiration to me. The irony of his going from being Superman to a quadriplegic man wasn't lost on anyone. Reeve took a message to the world about what was being learned regarding the needs of the disabled, as did Joni Eareckson Tada. The amount of money that they were able to collect for spinal cord research and outreach is staggering; as is the number of wheelchairs that Joni has been able to deliver to Third World communities. I respect and admire them both for their commitment "to the greater cause"… In addition, the way they live (or lived) their lives is a role model to each and every person with a disability, seen or unseen. Both of them exemplify courage, compassion, and commitment.

These individuals, and so many others I've not mentioned, were instrumental in helping me get to where I am today. It is true, "people who need people are the luckiest people in the world."

> *How important it is for us to recognize and celebrate*
> *our heroes and she-roes!*
>
> — Maya Angelou

Our friends fit into this category, too. I received the following forwarded e-mail about friendships:

Vitamin F

Why do I have a variety of friends who are all so different in character? How can I get along with them all? I think that each one helps to bring out a "different" part of me.

With one of them I am polite. I joke with another friend. I sit down and talk about serious matters with one. With another I laugh a lot — or cry a lot. I may have a cup of tea with one and enjoy a happy hour drink with another. I listen to one friend's problems. Then I listen to another one's advice for me.

My friends are all like pieces of a jigsaw puzzle. When completed, they form a treasure box. A treasure of friends! They are my friends who understand me better than myself, who support me through good days and bad days. We all pray together and for each other.

Doctors tell us that friends are good for our health. Dr. Oz calls them Vitamin Fs (for Friends) and counts the benefits of friends as essential to our well-being. Research shows that people in strong social circles have less risk of depression and terminal strokes.

Furthermore, it is said that if you enjoy Vitamin Fs regularly you can "be" up to 30 years younger than your real age. The warmth of friendship stops stress and even in your most intense moments, it decreases the chance of a cardiac arrest or stroke by 50%.

I'm so happy that I have a stock of Vitamin F!

In summary, we should value our friends and keep in touch with them. We should try to see the funny side of things and laugh together, and pray for each other in the tough moments.
Thank you for being one of my Vitamins!

— **Author Unknown**

LIVING IN COMMUNITY

*People who are in the best position for happiness
are the ones who have strong relationships
and "interconnected webs" of people on whom
they can depend for fun and support.*

— Fred Luskin

Since I have always been very social, it never surprised my family that I joined so many groups. I have also always believed in community. Communities are everywhere — family, friends, neighbors, work, church, and a bridge club or dinner group. All can be supportive, prayerful and oftentimes, a life-link.

Being part of a community is a beautiful thing. It feels inclusive and healthy and provides me the following:

- Accountability and Affirmation

- Compassion, Connection, and Celebration

- Encouragement and Empowerment

- Giving, Forgiving, Loving, Caring, and Sharing

- Support and Safety

Whenever I am part of a group, I feel enriched and enveloped by so many of these elements. My church family is a perfect example of the community attributes I have listed. I belong to several small groups within my church: small groups for sharing and praying, groups for outreach, groups for book and Bible study, dinner groups, and so on. I have shared, prayed, encouraged, and worshiped with these people for over 25 years. They are like family.

There are other communities that are important to me, too. For instance, I have always lived on a street where neighbors know one another. We share meals, take out each other's trash, transport one another to important events, or just wave to one another as we enter our houses. My colleagues at work form another group or community for which I am grateful. We have shared lesson plans, watched each other's classrooms, and covered for one another at meetings. We have shared meals, attended gatherings in each other's homes, and supported one another in times of crisis or grief.

———✿✿✿———

By far, the most important community with the greatest impact in my life is my family. I am lucky enough to have had a very close family growing up, which included both my mother's and father's extended families and my nuclear family. I had seven aunts and uncles and ten cousins. The families living in the San Francisco Bay Area gathered on Sundays and holidays to have dinner at my grandparents' home. We came to my San Diego grandparents every year for Thanksgiving while I was growing up, and I became even closer to everyone here when I moved down for college. Family memories fill my heart and my senses.

Christmas at my grandparents' was like the 1950s' Christmas specials for the Andy Williams Show. We would all get together and sing to my uncle's accordion carols (my grandpa sang in German) — it was always magical. But Easter was my favorite holiday. I'm sure my love for Easter started because my maiden name, Ostertag, means Easter Day in German. Beyond that, I loved getting a new dress and new shoes every year. The food and desserts were always traditional — and so delicious! There was always roasted goose for good luck and dessert that included special pudding eggs formed in real eggshells, then peeled and placed over a bed of green Jell-O (for grass). The camaraderie between the three generations was fun, carefree, and full of laughter. What great times we had!

Memories of my immediate family as I grew up are just as important. Every summer we took a vacation — a combination of driving and camping, with a few hotels in between. My sister and I could not wait to take real showers in the hotel and jump into the pools. We never wanted to bring separate friends — we had each other, and that was enough. These family trips gave me a foundation for my love of the outdoors for which I will be forever grateful...

At this point in time, I have lost my grandparents, my parents, and several aunts, uncles, and cousins. The nucleus of my family community, however, remains strong with my best friend and sister, Shirley, my brother-in-law, Bill, two nieces, Lindsay and Jamie, and their combined three kids. My great- nephews and niece, Brodie, Camden and JJ, fill in the space in my heart where I had anticipated grandkids. Luckily, they all live nearby — and I am blessed! My strong, loving family brings me incredible joy.

We have all known the long loneliness
and we have learned that the only solution is love
and that love comes with community.

— Dorothy Day

—⟨∿∿⟩—

I am a living example of how a community of people came together to do what no **one** person could have done alone — **and** it has a miraculous ending. Dr. Donna Brooks and Cathy Conheim have been friends of mine for nearly 30 years. They have offered to help me on a variety of levels, but never as much as in the instance I'm about to tell. It was recently recounted in *The Huffington Post* by BJ Gallagher when she interviewed Cathy for the article "Cathy Conheim: A Woman Who Knows How to Make Things Happen!"

BJ begins:

"Some people feel overwhelmed. Goals look so big; they don't know where to start. So some folks do nothing at all. They think, 'It's hopeless.' What would you say to them?"

"Start with one small step," Cathy replied. "Just because you can't do everything doesn't mean you can't do something."

"Some years ago, I took on a goal of raising $115,000 to buy a specially-equipped Freedom Van for a quadriplegic woman here in San Diego. She'd broken her neck in a terrible car accident, and her journey back from disaster had been hard and harrowing. When I met her, she had come far in rebuilding her life, but her 25-year-old van had finally given out, and she needed a replacement. The question was: how could a paralyzed school teacher ever buy such an expensive vehicle on her salary? She couldn't."

"So I committed to helping her. And you know what? Within 12 weeks, we raised the money — all by email, without using a single postage stamp! Here's how we did it: We sent out 50 emails to people we knew, people who trusted us. We explained the situation and told them, 'We promise you that every cent you send us will go to pay for the van. Not a penny will go to administration, not even postage!' We also asked them to go one step further — 'Send this email to ten people you know who trust you. Make the same promise to them that we made to you, and request that they pass along the request to ten more people who trust them.' This is important — we were building a **community of trust**. There are so many fundraising scams out there — we needed for people to trust us and to trust one another.

"We kept our promise, and they kept theirs. For the first two weeks, we received checks from people we knew. But by the third week, we were starting to get money from people whose names we didn't recognize. The network was working, and our community of trust was doing its job.

"We didn't need one person to give us $70,000 — we were happier to get 70,000 people to give just $1 each — a bigger community of donors and participants. People are glad to be part of something that makes a difference.

**If everybody picked just one other person to help,
the world would be transformed.**

— Cathy Conheim

Wanting to join the campaign, other people began fund-raising. My local Kiwanis club hosted a dinner raising $30,000; friends held "coffee socials," and an elementary school class had a bake sale to raise money. Small groups of people everywhere combined efforts to raise money for a new van for me. I could hardly believe what was happening! I needed a van that was way beyond my means, and a community of people — or rather multiple communities (to me, the universe) raised the money for it. I believe two major forces were at play here: God's grace, and my willingness to accept help from others.

Consider the following:

We humans are social beings.
We come into the world as the result of others' actions.
We survive here in dependence on others.
Whether we like it or not,
there is hardly a moment of our lives
when we do not benefit from others' activities.
For this reason it is hardly surprising
that most of our happiness
arises in the context of our relationships with others.

— Tenzin Gyatso, 14th Dalai Lama

The religious community is essential,
for alone our vision is too narrow to see
all that must be seen.
Together, our vision widens and strength is renewed.

— Mark Morrison-Reed

We don't accomplish anything in this world alone...
and whatever happens is the result
of the whole tapestry of one's life...

— Sandra Day O'Connor

I am of the opinion that my life belongs
to the whole community
and as long as I live, it is my privilege
to do for it whatever I can.
I want to be thoroughly used up when I die,
for the harder I work the more I live.

— George Bernard Shaw

PLEASE HELP

Refusing to ask for help when you need it is
refusing someone the chance to be helpful.

— Ric Ocasek

In an earlier chapter, I spoke about the benefits of being a person who needs people. My inability to do things for myself and my learned ability to ask for help has brought many new, interesting, and wonderful people into my life. Even if I were miraculously healed this instant, I would still find a way to "need people." It reminds me of the barn raising parties of the old West when the community came together to help a neighbor in need. It feels good to give, to receive, and to celebrate the camaraderie and friendship. That's how it feels when I ask for help.

Don't get me wrong, there are times when I feel like a bothersome pain in everyone's behind. When I need a channel turned, my head scratched, or a glass of water, it is difficult to be the one ALWAYS asking for help. I try to get around this by waiting until I need a couple of things so that when I ask my caregiver (or whoever is with me) to do something, they can accomplish two things at once. But that backfires sometimes, too. I have had people say to me that they dread getting my call because there will be so much that I want or need. I can't win!

Have you heard it said that asking for help is not "the American Way"? However, as I keep repeating *ad nauseam*, for someone as unable to help herself as I am, there is really no other way. It was time for me to tear down those blocks of privacy and pride that I had built up to prevent others from seeing the daily routines and rituals of my life, necessitated by the challenges of being a person with quadriplegia.

There are ways to organize and break down our needs into manageable requests. It's taken me a while to learn how to do this, and I would like to share some of the things I've learned.

Lori Deschene, author of *Tiny Buddha, Simple Wisdom for Life's Hard Questions,* is also the founder of the website and blog, Tiny Buddha (tinyBuddha.com). In one of her blogs, "Tiny Wisdom: On Asking for Help," she writes:

"We often think that admitting struggle is a sign of weakness, but we all struggle sometimes. We all get overwhelmed sometimes. We all need help sometimes. Acknowledging this is not a sign of weakness, but struggling alone is a choice to grow weak.

"We all need each other. No one is an island. The good news is that people really do care. Think about it. If someone you know were hurting, would you not offer your support? If people you know got into a tough situation, would you help them find a solution? You'd probably *want* them to come to you — to know that you care, and that they can trust and depend on you. Why not give them the opportunity to do the same for you? Why push yourself to your breaking point when there are people who'd be honored to help lighten your load?

"If you're carrying more than you can handle today, choose to let some of it go by letting someone else in. You may feel vulnerable asking for help, but wouldn't the world be a better place if we all learned to depend on each other?"

It's not the load that breaks you down;
it's the way you carry it.

— Lena Horne

Many people think "Help me" are words that imply weakness, help-less-ness. In actuality, the words "help me" can be two of the most powerful words in the English language. Knowing that you are asking for help makes you stronger, not weaker. It implies a strong sense of self to be able to understand and ask for what you need and still feel whole.

The phrase "Help me!" should not be linked to being a helpless person. When people see gaps in learning, help is what is needed. In fact, all education is really a form of "Help me": Help me learn to read, to do math, to use computers, history, language. All of these learned skills increase our sense of power in the world. Going without helpful learning is what leads to real helplessness and an inability to do anything for one's self.

My paralysis has made me truly helpless to sit up, walk, dress myself, and so many other physical things that I genuinely cannot do alone. But my mind, my ability to learn, my learned willingness to adapt to new situations, to hire the right people or to ask for help, and my commitment to finding new ways to accomplish outcomes — makes me helpless only in the narrowest physical sense. There are many who can move all of their limbs, but who have paralysis in their minds — and therefore cannot make their lives work. They might be considered more helpless than I. Many adults cannot say "Help me," I so they become helpless to be good parents, giving spouses, collegial coworkers, and a host of surprising and unexpected things they could learn if they did not see those words as a threat to their ego.

This prayer is appropriate here:

The Serenity Prayer
God grant me the serenity
to accept the things I cannot change;
the courage to change the things I can;
and the wisdom to know the difference.

— Attributed to Reinhold Niebuhr

I had to accept what I could not change and change what I could. The kicker on all of this, of course, is the wisdom to know the difference!

Do you resist asking for help until it's your last resort? Or, like me, do you feel like you are wearing out everyone around you?

In looking for solutions, I found an excellent article by business strategist, Shelly Cofoni. She extrapolated the main points from the book, *Mayday! Asking for Help in Times of Need*, by M. Nora Klaver. Below I have paraphrased parts of her article which pertain particularly to those of us who, for one reason or another, need so much help.

Klaver lists some of the reasons why people often delay a valid request for help until they have reached the point of desperation. She writes:

- We may not see the whole picture, so the help we ask for satisfies only part of our need.

- Our requests may be so unclear that others may not understand that we need help at all.

- We may ask for help too often without concern for our friends, family, and coworkers. Compassion fatigue becomes a real possibility for them.

The good news is that we **can** learn to ask for help, says Klaver. In fact, it can be fairly simple; but first, we've got to debunk some common cultural myths. A few examples are:

- **Asking for help makes you look weak or needy**. There's no shame in turning to others in true times of need. In fact, it's a sign of strength.

- **Asking for help can harm relationships.** Healthy relationships are about both *giving* and *receiving*.

- **Asking for help puts others in an awkward position.** It is human nature to offer help when you see someone in need—and it's no different when others see you in need.

- **Asking for help means the job might not get done right.** Refusing to ask because you fear losing control maintains the status quo. Let go and give your helpmate a chance to shine.

> *Don't be shy about asking for help.*
> *It doesn't mean you're weak,*
> *it only means you're wise.*
>
> — **Source Unknown**

Below, I have further simplified a few of Klaver's recommendations for growing in your ability to make strong and clear requests.

- *Clarify* exactly what you need. How many people will you need, and how much time will it take?

- *Expand* your list of helpmates; generate as many names of potential helpers as you can—even those who may say no. When creating your list, think about your specific need: will there be heavy lifting, does this person need a car, do they need computer skills?

- *Ask!* This is the step where you actually make the request.

- *Listen* to the response carefully to catch any underlying or emotional messages. If the answer is no, perhaps it is only because the person has a conflict at the time you need them, not that they are unwilling ever to help.

- *Thanks*. The final step is to say thank-you—whether your helpmate agrees to help you *or* not. Use the extremely helpful *Three Thanks Rule* by expressing your gratitude three times: 1. when the agreement is struck, 2. when the need has been met, and 3. when you next see your helper.

It took a while for me to feel comfortable, but I have found these pointers to be very helpful. It always seems easier to request help for someone other than myself. When Sandy was sick and undergoing therapy, there was no way I could take her to all her chemotherapy sessions. I created an e-mail list of people I thought might be able to help and sent out a request with dates and places to sign up to be one of her "Chemo Cabbies." The response was overwhelming.

Even now, I organize my projects into what seem to be easily managed chunks. Then I send out an e-mail with a list of "needs" and the approximate time I think it will take to accomplish. I ask my different communities of friends to let me know if they have time to work with me on any of my listed items. I am always pleasantly surprised at the number of people who can help. One of the things I've learned is to line up people who enjoy doing the particular task needed. For example, if I have a flower bed that needs weeding, I ask people who like to garden. When I needed someone to create a database listing Sandy's collection of 500 CDs, I asked people who are comfortable working with Excel.

As Klaver writes, "The more often you ask, the more comfortable you become." I did.

DISCOVERING JOY

If I keep a green bough in my heart,
the singing bird will come.

— **Chinese Proverb**

Planting flowers became a means of bringing joy into my life both literally and figuratively. Painting my house with bold yet feminine colors was the next step. I chose beautiful, life-giving colors (my living room has a raspberry wall) because they make me feel happy.

Color is like music —
It gives us a fast way to revive our senses
and awaken our emotions.

— Anna Maria Cimbal

This was translated from a handwritten sign on the side of a colorful building in Venice. It expresses the joy color brings me.

There are many ways of bringing joy into our lives: Being with family and friends has always been a happy reprieve from the rest of my daily activities. Next to people, the most profound joy I have found thus far in my new life has been working with service dogs. I have always loved dogs, but that love has evolved into a purpose, a passion, and a joy! My heart *calls* me into it.

A trained service dog has been at my side for more than 20 years. Dogs have always enriched my life, but it was not until I got Pacific from Tender Loving Canines Assistance Dogs in 2000 that I felt drawn to working with the organization that trains these dogs. I had an up-close and personal opportunity to watch how the dogs were trained as I worked with Pacific on my specific needs. I was mesmerized by how the trainers worked with the dogs and how adept the dogs were at learning precise, and many times life-saving, skills — I was hooked!

For the past 12 years, I have been a volunteer for TLCAD in one capacity or another. I knew that becoming a trainer was not for me. Many people with disabilities have trained their own service dog, but in my case I felt my paralysis was just too limiting. However, it was not hard to find other places within the organization to use my skills. I joined the Board of Directors and eventually became President. After rotating out of that position and off the board, I found myself writing curriculum, editing videos, and looking for donors and sponsors to join the TLCAD family. And recently, yet another new service dog organization is forming called Next Step Service Dogs, which offers me still other options and opportunities I very much look forward to pursuing!

My joy overflows every time I see a new person/dog partner-ship forming — watching the connection between each person and his or her dog is the purest of magic. I know that the trainers do their homework when putting a team together, but for me, it's more than that — "It's a God thing." God is not only being manifested in the love and joy between a dog and owner, His presence can be felt in the pairing of the two. They are "right" for one another on many levels and for many reasons — many that we may not know immediately.

Seeing the difference a dog can make in someone's life has captivated me in a way difficult to explain. I could fill pages with the stories I've seen unfold. I have witnessed a little girl with autism who, because of her dog, no longer has total, emotional meltdowns or escapes out the front door. I've seen a wounded warrior who can now go out in public because of the confidence his canine partner brings him. And I have been moved beyond words by the unsteady senior whose dog gives him balance and the ability to walk independently. I can never get enough of these stories. Sometimes I go on the websites of other Assistance Dog organizations just to read about the "teams" they create. There is joy in every story. God's love revealed!

Assistance Dogs can make all the difference in someone's life, and I get to witness it. What a privilege!

> *The only way to do great work is to love what you do.*
> *If you haven't found it yet, keep looking.*
> *Don't settle.*
> *As with all matters of the heart,*
> *you'll know when you find it.*
>
> — Steve Jobs

Working with Service Dogs is only one area where I find joy. I find happiness in other parts of my life as well — friends, family, and, of course, my garden. I love looking at photographs of beautiful places. Now that I can no longer travel easily, I also find joy in watching travel videos of places I'd like to go and in seeing the vacation photos of friends.

In reality, I'm always on the lookout for other ways to bring joy into my life. As I write this, I have just finished volunteer training

Think about what you love, really love about being alive,
about what lifts you up and makes you dance
and causes tears of joy to roll down your cheeks.
Commit yourself to that — and to joy.
You will see that it brings you out,
takes you to the doorstep of others,
and calls forth your voice, your strength, and your wisdom.

— Jan Phillips

EPILOGUE

Happiness has something to do with struggling, enduring, and accomplishing.

— George Sheehan

The conclusion of this book signifies quite an accomplishment for me. Writing a book was always something in the back of my mind for when I retired. In reality, I thought this would be like so many other projects that I've put up on a shelf and never finished. And now I've actually done it! Can you see me smiling?

This compilation of memories and stories would never have taken shape without prayer and reflection. Once I invited God into this endeavor, I feel that He set the course, took the reins, and led me through to the very end. I know beyond a shadow of a doubt that God organized my thoughts, spoke through me, and inspired my words.

One of the most satisfying pieces of putting all these stories together was being able to share so many of the quotes and poems that have been meaningful to me. I've kept a folder of these items for over 30 years, and this gave me a chance to go through each and every one of them, read them all — and once again be touched by their emotion and wisdom.

On a separate note:

It always surprises me when people don't expect me to smile or look happy sitting in this wheelchair. In fact, sometimes they don't even expect me to be able to speak clearly. To me, it is wonderful that my smile sometimes attracts people to me even more than my service dog! I think my smile says to people, "I enjoy life!" — and it often evokes a curiosity that leads to conversation. It is unfortunate that many people think that a disability and a smile are an oxymoron. It is a joy to show people that it is not. I know that my smile is God-given, and I'm honored to let His light shine through me.

—◦◦◦—

May there be peace within you today. May you trust that you are exactly where you are meant to be. May you not forget the infinite possibilities that are born of faith. May you use the gifts that you have received, and pass on the love that has been given to you. May you be content with yourself just the way you are.

Let this knowledge settle into your bones, and allow your soul the freedom to sing, dance, praise and love. Peace, contentment, faith, and joy are gifts that are available for each and every one of us.

— Saint Therese of Lisieux

Amen!

WORKS CITED

Anderson, Mac., and Gallagher, BJ., *Learning to Dance in the Rain.* Naperville: Simple Truths, 2009. Print.

Borges, Jorge Luis. *Comes the Dawn.* Authorship disputed.

Carter-Scott, Cherie. *If Life Is a Game… These Are the Rules.* Naperville: Simple Truths, 2010. Print.

Cofini, Shelly. *When Do You Ask for Help?* www.shellycofini.com

Deschene, Lori. *Tiny Buddha, Simple Wisdom for Life's Hard Questions.* San Francisco: Conari, 2012. Print.

Emmons, Robert A. *Thanks! How the New Science of Gratitude Can Make You Happier.* New York: Houghton Mifflin, 2007. Print.

Fox, Paula. *Courage Doesn't Always Roar.* San Francisco: Conari Press, 2009. Print.

Fankl, Viktor. *Man's Search for Meaning.* Boston: Beacon Press, 2006. Print.

Klaver, M. Nora. *Mayday! Asking For Help in Times of Need.* San Francisco: Berrett-Kohler, 2007. Print.

Kubler-Ross, Elizabeth. *On Death and Dying.* New York: Scribner, 1969. Print.

Listeners, Two. *God Calling*. New Alresford: John Hunt, 1999. Print.

Mortenson, Alice Hansche. *I Needed the Quiet: Selected Poems*. Kansas City: Beacon Hill, 1978. Print.

Rambali, Paul. *Barefoot Runner*. Blackstock Mews: Serpent's Tail, 2007. Print.

Tada, Joni Eareckson. *Pearls of Great Price*. Grand Rapids: Zondervan, 2006. Print.

Valens, Evans G., *The Other Side of the Mountain*, New York: Harper Perennial, 1989 (first print 1966), Print.

Vujicic, Nick. *Life Without Limits*. New York: Doubleday, 2010. Print.

Seligman, Martin E. P., *Learned Optimism: How to Change Your Mind and Your Life*. New York: Simon & Schuster, 1990. Print.

I want to order _____ copy(ies) @ $14.00 of *The Up Side of Down*
by Christine Timmins

Name _____

Address _____

City _____ State _____ Zip _____

E-mail _____ Phone (for questions only) _____

Enclosed is my ❏ check or ❏ money order in the amount of

$_____ payable to Christine Timmins

Please add $6 postage for 1–3 books and $12 for 4–12 books.
Contact me: chris@braidedstreams.com or
P.O. Box 421191, San Diego, CA 92142

I want to order _____ copy(ies) @ $14.00 of *The Up Side of Down*
by Christine Timmins

Name _____

Address _____

City _____ State _____ Zip _____

E-mail _____ Phone (for questions only) _____

Enclosed is my ❏ check or ❏ money order in the amount of

$_____ payable to Christine Timmins

Please add $6 postage for 1–3 books and $12 for 4–12 books.
Contact me: chris@braidedstreams.com or
P.O. Box 421191, San Diego, CA 92142

I want to order _____ copy(ies) @ $14.00 of *The Up Side of Down*
by Christine Timmins

Name _____

Address _____

City _____ State _____ Zip _____

E-mail _____ Phone (for questions only) _____

Enclosed is my ❏ check or ❏ money order in the amount of

$_____ payable to Christine Timmins

Please add $6 postage for 1–3 books and $12 for 4–12 books.
Contact me: chris@braidedstreams.com or
P.O. Box 421191, San Diego, CA 92142

Made in the USA
San Bernardino, CA
11 December 2012